Copyright © 2016 by Neil T Stacey

All rights reserved. No part of this publication may be reproduced, distributed, or transmitted in any form or by any means, including photocopying, recording, or other electronic or mechanical methods, without the prior written permission of the publisher, except in the case of brief quotations embodied in critical reviews and certain other non-commercial uses permitted by copyright law. For permission requests, write to the publisher, addressed "Attention: Permissions Coordinator," at the address below.

Sweatshop Press

A41 No.3 Renaissance Drive
Crown Mines
Johannesburg
2092

This book is loosely based on real events and is set at real locations. For the international version, the University of the Witwatersrand has been renamed to West Rand University because foreigners understandably mispronounce 'Wits'.

The individual characters are entirely fictitious.

I would also be remiss to not point out that the depiction of the Wits SRC as ineffectual and apathetic is specific to the time period portrayed in this book. In more recent years, the SRC has done some incredible work on behalf of disadvantaged students.

Kill Time or Die Trying

A WARP club novel by:

Neil T Stacey

KILL TIME OR DIE TRYING

Chapter 1

Jamie Rogers: Just got my Matric results, all the hard work paid off. Looking forward to growing as a person in my time at West Rand University
   10 January, 2010
     3 people like this
       1 Comment: **Elliot Rogers:** I'm not paying for personal growth, son. You're going to West to become a lawyer so that I can retire

*

"Galloping poop noodles!" yelled Jamie, slapping his palm on the rim of the steering wheel. Jarryd stopped what he was doing to stare at him.

"Just say fuck like a normal person," said Jarryd. "Normal people swear. Besides," he continued, picking up the Nintendo DS he'd dropped on the ground just outside the car door. "That wouldn't have happened if your passenger seat wasn't six inches deep in comic-books."

"Just chuck everything in the back and get in," said Jamie. "Or we'll both be late."

"I thought you'd lost this," Jarryd said, examining the handheld console as he climbed in. "Mom bought you a new one and everything." While waiting for the garage door to open, Jamie glanced sideways, noting with consternation that his fifteen year old brother would soon be taller than him. Three years younger than Jamie, Jarryd shared his pale skin, blue eyes and shaggy blonde hair. Until recently he had also shared Jamie's plump cheeks and soft jaw line.

"What's wrong with 'galloping poop noodles'?" Jamie asked as he pulled out of the driveway. "I'm trying it out as an alternative to swearing."

"No," said Jarryd, pulling on his seatbelt. "No no no. I think it's actually worse than swearing. I pictured things I'm not comfortable with. Never use it again." Jamie shrugged.

"I'll reserve that one specifically for you then," he said with a grin.

"I already think you're a dork," said Jarryd with a shrug. "You won't be doing any damage as long as you don't say it in public."

"You know," said Jamie sarcastically. "It's great having a brother looking out for me like this. Like the time you told everyone at school that I was in a special hospital being treated for baldness."

"I had to come up with something," said Jarryd. "I couldn't tell them you were playing the tuba with a brass band."

"Yeah sure, but your friends are superhumanly stupid," said Jamie. "They'll grow up believing there are special hospitals for baldness." Soon after, Jamie pulled up alongside Jarryd's school. Jarryd jumped out before the car had fully stopped, dragging his overloaded backpack out behind him. As Jarryd drew out of sight, Jamie surreptitiously reached into the back seat for the Nintendo DS and turned it over to check if his Pokemon Diamond cartridge was still in the slot. Seeing that it was, Jamie gave a fist pump of triumph. This would be his first day at West Rand University and it was off to a great start.

Jamie parked across the road from West and stepped out of his car, squinting in the bright sunlight as he looked over the road at the lengthy queue at the access turnstile. He strode across the road to join the queue, backpack secure over both shoulders and student card at the ready in his pocket. He pulled the DS from his backpack and flicked the power switch hopefully. No response. No sign of life left in the battery.

Disappointed but not surprised, Jamie glanced down at his watch. It was orientation week and his first seminar was still a whole hour away. He had plenty of time and the queue was barely moving so he just phased out, shuffling forward rhythmically every time the RFID reader at the turnstile beeped in recognition of a valid student card. He was eventually jarred out of his reverie when the line abruptly halted and he stopped up short, mere millimetres from bumping into the guy in front of him.

A long drawn out beep sounded up ahead. Someone's card wasn't on the system yet and the RFID reader was rejecting it. Jamie shifted uncomfortably as the harsh beep was repeated. After a third unsuccessful attempt, the unlucky student stepped aside and let the queue past, joining a small crowd who had already suffered the same fate. They had gotten their first taste of West bureaucracy before they'd even made it onto the premises.

By the time Jamie reached the front of the queue, perspiration was creeping down his neck. It was a hot day, but more than that he was nervous that his card might be rejected, embarrassing him in front of the long line of impatient students. As Jamie pulled his brand new student card from his pocket it slipped from his sweaty fingers and fell on the other side of the gate. Jamie quickly crouched and stretched an arm between the bars. His outstretched fingertips came agonisingly close to his card. Jamie winced in humiliation and tried to ignore the shouts of impatience from behind him.

It occurred to Jamie to ask for help from the other side of the turnstile but the last person through was already out of earshot and hurrying away. Hearing swearing behind him, Jamie made one more effort, straining against the bars as he stretched for every inch. Suddenly a buzzer sounded, and he fell flat on his face as the turnstile gave way.

"Now pass me your card," said a female voice behind him. "So I can swipe in." Jamie scrambled the rest of the way through the gate, snatched up his card and handed it through the bars to a brightly smiling brunette girl. "I suppose I should have warned you I was going to do that. I'm sorry, I didn't realise you'd fall," she continued, pocketing her own student card. The RFID reader buzzed satisfactorily as she waved Jamie's card in front of it. Jamie stood by sheepishly as she walked through and handed him his card. "I'm Tarryn, by the way." She extended a hand, which Jamie shook.

"Jamie. Sorry about the hold-up back there. I can imagine how stupid I looked."

"I'm not sure you can," said Tarryn, shaking her head slowly. She looked a couple of years older than Jamie, with curly brown hair framing a warmly smiling face. She was quite short, with bright hazel eyes. "Don't worry about it," Tarryn went on. "Everyone expects first-years to be helpless. Which way are you going?" she asked him as she started walking again, straight uphill along the main road through the campus. Jamie caught himself glancing down at Tarryn's chest and flushed red with embarrassment, but she didn't seem to notice. Feeling anxious and embarrassed, Jamie quickly pointed off to his right.

"I need to go to West Campus," he blurted out. "You know, law faculty."

"Nice meeting you," said Tarryn, walking backwards for a few steps as she waved goodbye. As he veered in the other direction, Jamie touched the fingers of his left hand to the palm of his right and was mortified to discover that his hand was even clammier than he had feared.

Great, he thought to himself. *First girl I meet and I don't just fall on my face, I reach out with a hand that feels like a baby squid.*

*

Jamie ducked through a tunnel and made his way toward West Campus and the law faculty buildings. The sprawling Main Campus of West is divided in two by a freeway. On one side lies East Campus, home to the faculties of Science, Engineering and Art. On the other side lies West Campus, home to the faculty of Commerce, Law and Management. East and West campus are joined by two main thoroughfares: a tunnel underneath the freeway, located at the bottom end of the campus, and Amic deck, a broad paved platform spanning the freeway at the top end. By the time Jamie reached the tunnel he was walking alone, the main stream of students continuing uphill toward the University's main buildings on East Campus.

It was the first day of orientation week and Jamie's first destination was the Oliver Schreiner Law Building, where most of the law school's lectures took place. He could expect this to be his second home for the next four years or so. If his transformation into a public prosecutor were to take place, this building was where it would happen. Jamie made his way to the front desk to ask where he should be going for his o-week lectures.

"What does it say on your timetable?" said the receptionist, not even looking up from the magazine she was paging through.

"Well, it says I've got the Dean's address at 9:00, then it says it's in OLS 16B. What does that mean?"

"I have no idea," said the receptionist, sounding bored. "You should try asking at faculty office, it's in CLM." Jamie stared at her. "Commerce, Law and Management," she said. "It's the faculty you're registered in," said the receptionist, rolling her eyes. She sighed in boredom and gave Jamie directions.

Jamie followed those directions to the letter for as long as he could, eventually coming to the perimeter fence. Turning back the way he had come, Jamie spent a frustrating fifteen minutes checking out all the nearby buildings.

Eventually finding the Commerce, Law and Management building, Jamie was greeted by a queue. Well, ignored by a queue. West has twenty seven thousand students, and Jamie was beginning to feel like he was destined to stand behind each and every one of them.

"Why are you here?" was the response of the receptionist, whose facial expression suggested that he hated his life, his job and, most especially, the mole on Jamie's forehead. "Try the Law Building, that's where your department is."

"They sent me here," Jamie protested, nervously pulling his fringe down to cover the offending blemish. "I'm just looking for some place called OLS 16B."

"Maybe OLS stands for Oliver Schreiner?" said the receptionist, shrugging. "Go see if there's a 16B in there."

Jamie returned to Oliver Schreiner only to discover that Room 16B was a women's bathroom. Jamie made use of room 16A to relieve himself of his morning coffee.

Unwilling to try the queue again, Jamie checked his watch. 8:40. Twenty minutes left before he missed the Dean's address. It would take longer than that to reach the front of either of the reception queues. Jamie had to gamble. He pulled out the map of the Main Campus he'd been given when he'd enrolled, and started searching for a building which could be abbreviated as OLS. Finding none, he resorted to asking a passer-by for help. There were plenty of passers-by, but it took Jamie several minutes to identify one that he felt comfortable approaching, a kindly-looking middle-aged woman who reminded him a bit of his mom. Jamie walked up to her with a friendly smile.

"Hi there," he said, trying desperately to make eye-contact with the woman, who lowered her head and ignored him, staring intently at a phone that clearly wasn't even turned on. "I'm new here and I'm looking for the law faculty's O-Week lectures," Jamie persisted as the woman proceeded to tap away at buttons on her phone which was still clearly turned off.

"Hey man," a voice said from just over Jamie's shoulder. It was one of the passersby that Jamie had elected to pass over. In this case, an ebony-skinned guy in his twenties that Jamie had eliminated for being too muscular to be friendly. "I couldn't help overhearing," he continued. "If you're having trouble with your O-Week schedule, your best bet is the enrolment centre in Senate House, they'll help you out."

Jamie thanked him profusely, but his shoulders slumped. Senate House was at the very top of East Campus, fifteen minutes walk from where Jamie was standing, and all of it uphill.

With time running out, Jamie laboured all the way up to the enrolment centre, his thighs beginning to burn from straining up the slope. Finally arriving at the Reception desk, he found more queue than he could cope with. He stared glumly at his watch, realising that he was bound to miss the speech.

*

Almost an hour later, Jamie still couldn't find his orientation group but at that point he'd have settled for shade and somewhere to sit. Wandering aimlessly away from Senate House, he walked past Central Block, one of West's oldest and most historic buildings, eventually spotting a large marquee in the middle of a quad. The sign at the entrance read 'Clubs and Societies Recruitment' but Jamie barely noticed it as he stepped into the blessed shade of the marquee. A voice called out to Jamie as he looked around for a seat.

"It's only 10am, and you're already sunburnt," said a voice. "You're pretty much one of us already, just sign this form and make it official." A pen was thrust into his hand and he found himself signing something.

Just like that, Jamie found himself an unwitting member of WARP.

The club's recruiting booth was littered with an eclectic array of Warhammer figurines and Manga, backed by a cascade of game and movie posters.

Jamie subsided gratefully into a chair at the club's table. It had an uncomfortable warmth, but Jamie just basked in the relief of resting his legs and feet.

He found himself staring across at the deranged grin of a fat man with a tangled beard and unkempt hair well past his shoulders.

"Howdy, filthy first-year. The guy who signed you up is James, and I'm Bernard." Bernard was about to say more when he was cut off by James.

"And yes," James said. "He is as stupid as he looks."

"But more handsome," Bernard replied, stroking his beard. His thumb got stuck and he yanked it free with a wince.

"That doesn't even make sense," said James, whose smooth face could have been described as cherubic were it not for his attempt at a contemptuous scowl. "I take it back," he said, turning to Jamie. "Bernard is much dumber than he looks."

"I find that hard to believe," said Jamie kindly. The third WARP member behind sitting behind the stall was lean and wiry with an angular face and he glanced over at Jamie with vivid blue eyes.

"You say that," he said. "Because, yes, Bernard is unbelievably dumb-looking. But we're talking about a man who grew a beard just so that he could eat without a bib for the first time."

"In my defence, I was only nine at the time," said Bernard. "And don't mind Nathan, he's always like this."

"No," said Nathan. "Sometimes I am asleep."

"And that hasn't been proven," added James. "Now get out of that seat, newbie. It's for people who haven't signed up yet. You do get a free t-shirt, though. You can collect it next Monday."

"Uh, thanks," said Jamie uncertainly, standing up. "By the way, do you guys know where OLS is?"

"Right over there," said James, pointing to a squat concrete structure off to Jamie's left, further from Yale

Road. "The Oppenheimer Life Sciences building. Home to the worst lecture venues on campus."

Jamie weaved his way through the crowd and made his way toward the OLS building. There was a one hour break between orientation seminars; he could make it in time for the second one.

Ten minutes into the second seminar, Jamie no longer felt bad about missing the first one. The lecture venue was below-ground, dimly lit and barely ventilated. The only objective of the seminar seemed to be explaining vaguely that there were libraries on campus and that maybe it would be a good idea to use them. The lecturer was at a loss about how to stretch this to forty five minutes.

But he managed, somehow.

When a fifteen-minute break was announced, Jamie slung his bag over his shoulder and made for the door, jostled by a crowd with the same idea. He had a lot of time to kill, now that he'd decided to skip the rest of those seminars.

Jamie decided he could use the extra time to go buy his textbooks. Blinking in the bright sun, Jamie checked his campus map.

Not a word about the bookshop.

There was only one place he'd gotten decent directions that whole day. No reason not to go back there.

*

Jamie made his way back to the clubs and societies marquee. The crowds had mostly dissipated and the

WARP table had changed occupancy since he'd last seen it. Nathan was still there, though, looking bored. With him was a familiar face:

"Hey, Jamie right?" Tarryn asked as he reached the table. "Are you interested in joining WARP?"

"I signed up earlier," he replied.

"Congratulations," she said, smiling broadly. "And welcome to WARP. I hope you enjoy your time with us, I'm sure you'll fit right in. Take a seat."

Nathan looked at her askance and made gagging motions. She shot him a venomous glance and then motioned for Jamie to sit down. He gladly complied, relieved to be off his feet.

"So," said Jamie, curious about what he'd signed up for. "What does WARP actually do?"

"We play tabletop games," said Tarryn. "We also watch anime and read comics."

"We play card games," added Nathan.

"And console games," said Tarryn.

"One time we killed a dude," added Nathan.

"We host monthly LANs," said Tarryn. "But mostly we're a social group that hangs out and relaxes in our club-room. And don't mind Nathan; he's always like this."

*

Chapter 2

Jamie Rogers is now friends with **Tarryn Park**, **Bernard Cronje**, **James Green** and **Nathan Hillary**
Jamie Rogers: O-week wasn't quite what I expected. Well, I've got all of my textbooks, so I can just stay at home and get a head start on my courses! Next week, university starts for real!
      11 January 2010

*

By the time Jamie's alarm clock rang, he was already wide awake and sitting up in his bed, sipping a glass of water.

He pulled open his curtains, squinting in anticipation of bright sunlight. Instead, dark clouds dominated the sky. As Jamie stared down from his second-storey window, a light drizzle began to mottle the road with darker spots. Jamie heard the sound of the front door opening, and saw Jarryd dart across the lawn, his lanky frame hunched against the rain. Jarryd skidded to a halt at the front gate and leaned down to pick up a damp newspaper before charging back toward the house.

Jamie smiled slightly as he waited, silently counting down in his head.

"Jarryd!" The sound of his mother's voice rang through the house. "How many times do I have to tell you to wipe your feet?" As usual, Jarryd was already charging up the stairs back to his bedroom by the time he mumbled an apology. "And tell your brother that breakfast is ready." As usual, Jarryd didn't bother to knock, instead just throwing open Jamie's door.

"Hey fatty," said Jarryd, standing in the doorway, glancing around Jamie's bedroom. His mouth quirked in amusement as his eyes stopped briefly at Jamie's new Sonic the Hedgehog poster, laid out on his desk since he hadn't yet found a spot for it on his wall. "Breakfast's ready," said Jarryd. "It's pancakes, though, so you should skip it." Before Jamie could reply, Jarryd slammed the door shut again, and carried on to his own bedroom, just past Jamie's.

Jamie grimaced. He was barely overweight, just a little flabby, but that was enough for his younger brother. It didn't help that Jarryd, three years younger, was very rapidly closing in on Jamie's six feet of height and already carrying more muscle.

Jamie piled some pancakes onto a plate and poured a glass of orange juice, eager to get to West bright and early for his first day of classes. His dad, Elliot Rogers, was sitting across from him at the kitchen table, reading the newspaper, with his collar open and his tie draped over the back of his chair. Tall and well-built with slightly greying temples, Elliot was a distinguished-looking man when he took the effort to neaten himself up. He had recently been promoted to Deputy Headmaster at St. John's College, the upmarket private school Jamie and Jarryd had attended since early childhood.

"So Jamie," said Elliot, folding up his newspaper and laying it down on the table. "I was wondering why you didn't go in for the rest of O-Week." Jamie shrugged in response.

"Those seminars seemed a bit pointless," he said. "The lecturers didn't seem to know what they were talking about so I figured I'd be better off reading up on my own."

"That's fair enough," Elliot responded. "But in my day there were some quite good parties during O-Week. University isn't just about studying, son. You need to get out and meet people." Elliot paused. "Not that academics aren't your main priority," he added. "Tuition fees aren't cheap, you know."

*

"So who's excited for their first criminal law class?" Jamie asked, looking around at his classmates as he walked into the lecture venue. A few of his classmates glanced at him with disinterest, while others actually seemed annoyed by his excitement. Most just ignored him. One voice did answer him, though, with a loud shout from just over his left shoulder:

"First and **only** class, hell yeah!" It was James. "This Johnson guy doesn't take attendance," James continued. "We head in, we get the pack of notes for the semester, and Monday mornings are free from here on out." Questions flooded Jamie's mind, but his mouth froze, and he found himself following James, who walked to a desk at the front of the class where students were collecting packs of notes. James grabbed two packs, handing one to Jamie and shoving the other under his arm.

"Come on Brad," said James, clapping Jamie on the shoulder as he walked right through the lecture venue to the door on the other side. "I'll show you where you get the best coffee on campus."

Jamie's feet were out the door before he really knew what was happening. He found himself trotting to keep up with James, who was headed straight for the tunnel leading to East Campus.

"Hey, you just walked past the coffee shop," Jamie pointed out. James shook his head.

"It's a shop," he said. "But whatever they sell is not coffee. No, Brad, we're going to the Matrix."

"Seems a bit far, just to get coffee. And my name's Jamie," said Jamie. James turned to him and narrowed his eyes, attempting to look menacing. His curly blond hair and baby blue eyes would have undercut his effort, even if scowling didn't bring out deep dimples on his cheeks.

"A half a mile is a short way to go for real coffee," said James. "And we'll see about the name."

They emerged from the tunnel just as the cloud cover broke and bright sunlight flooded the parking lot below the Matrix.

The Matrix, the student centre of West, was really a miniature mall, and the one destination that could reliably draw B.Com students away from the sparkling fountains and rolling lawns of West Campus and into the dreary concrete landmass east of Yale Road. Jamie followed James through the front entrance.

Off to their left were the financial powerhouses of the Matrix: the Walton's stationery store and the Jetline print shop. Try as they might, Apple and Amazon will not soon eliminate paper and pens from universities. And a print shop? They might as well be holding students up by their ankles and shaking them down. Printing could be done more cheaply in the libraries, but only the most daring would risk a tight deadline queuing behind random strangers praying for paper and ink to hold out.

"Filthy grease vendors," said James, waving a hand dismissively at the row of fast-food chains lining the corridor to the right.

"If you're strapped for cash, get food from the Seven-Eleven on the far side, by the stairs. That way you at least get your diabetes at a discount. If money isn't an issue, get real food at Nino's. That's where we're going now."

Right in the middle of the grease vendors, stuck between a Chinese place and a burger joint, was an Italian Cafe.

"Now, it's a good thing we're here during lectures," said James as he walked up to the till. "Or there'd be a queue. Two coffees, Mario," James said to the middle-aged proprietor behind the counter. "And something for my friend," he continued with a grin, nudging Jamie in the ribs "No, no, I'm kidding of course. Nothing for him." Nevertheless, James handed Jamie a cup of coffee. James closed his eyes as he savoured his first sip.

"Uh," said Jamie, seizing the opportunity to finally speak. "If you're in my class, then you're a first-year, right? How do you know this place so well?"

"First year of law," amended James. "I did Fine Arts for a while, but I decided that I'd rather be employable, so I switched."

"He did Accounting for a year in between," added a familiar voice. Tarryn had walked into the coffee shop.

"That was a gap year!" protested James. "I just registered for a couple of courses so I could stay on my mom's medical aid as a student."

"Sure James. Sure," said Tarryn, smiling wryly and shaking her head slowly. She then nodded in Jamie's direction. "Are you taking Jamie up to the club-room?"

"Brad," corrected James. "And no, I'm staying away from the club-room for a bit, Seth's been looking for me. Apparently he has paperwork."

"You're president of WARP now, James," said Tarryn. "You have to sign off on the budget."

"The less stuff I sign, the less stuff I can get blamed for," said James. "Come on Brad, we've got textbooks to photocopy. You did buy the textbooks, right?"

Chapter 3

Jamie Rogers: "Risk more than others think is safe. Care more than others think is wise. Dream more than others think is practical. Expect more than others think is possible."
    13 February, 2010
       1 comment: **Jarryd Rogers**: "Eat more than others think is healthy."

*

"No lecture today," announced Professor Ditko. "Just hand in your assignments and you can go." Jamie eyes widened. Assignment? What assignment?

Was there a notice-board somewhere that he didn't know about, that he was supposed to check for assignments? Or was it because he hadn't checked his student email? There must be some system for giving out assignments. They'd probably explained it during those o-week seminars he'd skipped.

It was only the second week of term, and he was going to get a zero. How would he tell his parents that he was failing already? Jamie stared at his desk, nightmare scenarios running through his head. Holding his head in his hands, he failed to notice that the rest of the class was just as confused as he was, if not quite as terrified.

"Prof, you didn't give us an assignment," said someone at the front of the class. Jamie didn't notice. He was lost in a reverie of horror. Mom would kill him. Jarryd would never let him live it down. Failing first-year. How could this happen?

"What?" asked Professor Ditko, confused. He rubbed a hand through his scruffy hair. "Are you sure?" Most of the class nodded. He began rummaging in his papers, and sighed loudly when he didn't find what he was looking for. "Ok, looks like I don't have anything for you at the moment. Your homework is to read fifty pages of any textbook. And someone see if that blond guy is ok, he looks like he's having a stroke."

James patted Jamie on the shoulder and helped him to his feet. They walked together out of the door.

"You need to learn to relax, Brad," said James.

"Jamie," corrected Jamie.

"I know just the place," James continued regardless. "Time for your first visit to the WARP club-room, Brad. Now, don't worry that you aren't a member of the club, it'll be fine as long as you're with me."

"I am a member," said Jamie. "You signed me up yourself."

"You sure?" said James, looking puzzled. "Even better."

"So where is this club-room?" Brad asked as they walked through the tunnel and onto East Campus.

"Top floor of the Matrix," replied James. "Prime real-estate." On the far side of the Matrix, away from the print shop, past Nino's cafe and just next to the Seven Eleven, there was a staircase. James grinned in anticipation as they climbed.

"I haven't actually been in WARP since O-week," he said. "It'll be interesting to see how things are going there." After climbing two stories, they took a right turn and walked along a dim corridor, lined with doors and security gates. As they walked, Jamie peered at the placards marking the doors, trying to make sense of the acronyms on them.

'SAUJS'. Jamie figured that one out from a poster next to the door. It was the South African Union of Jewish Students.

'DAM'. A sticker on the door showing a wheelchair led Jamie to guess that the 'D' was for Disability or Disabled. The 'M' probably stood for Movement, which Jamie didn't find the least bit ironic.

'PYA'. Progressive Youth Alliance. Jamie remembered that one from a pamphlet he'd been given during O-Week.

'BSS'. Jamie hadn't the faintest clue what that one meant.

'SRC'. That one was easy, Students Representative Council, this was the office of the elected student council.

'Trespassers will be eaten' proclaimed the placard on the final door. James opened it and walked in. Jamie followed him in, and got his first look at the WARP clubroom.

The room was effectively split in two by a support pillar in the centre of it. In one section of the room, couches surrounded a coffee table, and in the other, a motley collection of office chairs surrounded a large, cluttered desk. The group on the couches were deep in a conversation led by a black-haired guy who looked a year or two older than Jamie's nineteen. His name was Seth and his pale, gangly appearance imprinted itself on Jamie as typical of a longtime WARP member.

Also on a couch was Bernard, the overweight, heavily bearded man he'd met at the stall during o-week. He was talking enthusiastically to a glassy-eyed blonde girl looking desperate for an excuse to leave.

A similar pattern repeated itself in the group sitting on office chairs around a table: slightly older members who seemed to wear the club-room like a second skin, and obvious outsiders stranded in a hostile land. The older members seemed to follow an unspoken dress code of black t-shirts and jeans.

"So who failed what, and how bad?" James asked loudly, looking around the room.

The first to respond to James's question was Seth. He turned slowly towards James, careful not to spill the laptop propped up on his knees. He tilted his head quizzically, and Jamie noted that Seth was one of the palest people he had ever seen, a fact which was further highlighted by his coal-black hair and dark brown eyes.

"James, what are you even studying this year? And where were you last week? You were supposed to sign off on the club budget. I had to do it instead."

"Yes you did, Seth. Yes you did," replied James.

"You didn't answer any of his questions," said Nathan, who was one of a group playing a complicated-looking card game at the large desk. "Are you doing an actual degree this year?"

"I'll have you know," said James, drawing himself up to his full, if average, height. "That I am studying law."

"That's three different faculties in three years," Nathan said. "If you could just get into engineering you could go for the full set. So who's the new guy?" he asked, nodding in Jamie's direction.

"This is Brad," James replied proudly.

"Jamie," corrected Jamie. The club members looked at Jamie speculatively.

"He doesn't seem quite manly enough for a Brad," said Nathan after sizing Jamie up.

"He'll grow into it," said James. "And it's short for Bradford, not Bradley." Bernard nodded his approval, and after a few moments, so too did Nathan and Seth.

"Brad it is, then," announced Seth. "Officially."

"Jamie," corrected Brad, thinking that this was just a phase and that they would soon get back to calling him Jamie.

*

"I've never even **seen** this Dr. Johnson, I'm not sure we should be skipping all his classes," said Brad. It was Monday and he was once again with James in the clubroom instead of Dr. Johnson's Customary Law lecture.

It was one week after Brad's first visit and the clubroom was far less crowded than during his first visit. He had a couch to himself, the other was occupied by another first year, a tall slender Indian with a soft voice and reserved mannerisms. The club had named him Kevin.

Seth, Bernard and James were playing a convoluted board game at the large table. Bernard didn't seem to know the rules, so Seth was helping him, which amounted to playing on his behalf. James didn't know the rules either, but he wouldn't admit it so Seth was thrashing him from two sides.

"Relax, Brad. Johnson lectures straight out of the notes," said James, grimacing at the board. "Going to the class would be counter-productive, your brain would just start associating those concepts with boredom, and you'd end up falling asleep in an exam." As he said this last, he looked at Bernard pointedly.

"That was one time!" protested Bernard. "I still think Nathan spiked my coffee with something."

"Nah," said Seth. "Nathan's a bastard, but he wouldn't do that." Seth paused for a moment. "He has too much respect for coffee."

"How do you guys put up with Nathan, anyway?" Brad asked. "He seems pretty abrasive." As Brad said this, the small fridge in the far corner of the club-room popped open, and Nathan levered himself out of it.

"I'll not stay here to be insulted," he said, blue eyes bright with anger. "Good day." he finished, marching toward the door indignantly.

"Were you in there the whole time?" Brad asked.

"I said good day!" said Nathan, slamming the door behind him. Brad looked around the room. The only other person who seemed surprised was Kevin, who had walked over to the fridge to swing the door open and closed a few times, peering in disbelief at the cramped interior.

"Yeah, that happens from time to time," said Seth. "You'll get used to it. Nathan's nothing to worry about." Seth flinched as he said this, because the club-room door swung open just as he finished. When it was Tarryn who walked through the door rather than Nathan, he relaxed visibly. Kevin, meanwhile, was still inspecting the interior of the fridge.

"Guys, you know this thing is on, right?" he said. "There's someone's lunch in there."

"Probably Bernard's," said Tarryn. "If you're feeling charitable you could scoop some of the mayonnaise off his sandwiches, help keep him alive a bit longer," she continued, walking up to the table. "Hi James," she said, peering at the game pieces in front of James. "Looks like you're losing. To Bernard." Bernard stroked his beard and smiled gleefully as he reached for one of his pieces. Seth slapped his hand away with a glare and moved something different for him.

"Hi Jamie," said Tarryn, rounding the pillar in the middle of the room and sitting on the couch next to Brad.

"Brad," corrected James. Tarryn rolled her eyes, then smiled apologetically at Brad.

"They do this to all the first-years now," she said. "Nathan renamed one guy and it stuck, now everybody wants a chance to name someone. Well, this room has seen worse nicknames than Bradley, I'll tell you that much"

"It's short for Bradford," corrected Seth.

"Of course it is," she replied. Her eyes rested for a moment on Kevin. "So what are you calling this one?" she asked.

"Kevin," said James.

"Is that short for Kevinford?" Tarryn asked sweetly.

Chapter 4

Jamie "Bradford" Rogers is now friends with **Suresh "Kevinford" Singh** and **Seth Feynman**
15 March, 2010

*

"I don't get it," said Jarryd, pulling against his seatbelt as he leaned forward from the back-seat of Jamie's car. "Why does he call you Brad?"

"It's short for Bradford," added Kevin, from the passenger seat beside Jamie.

"Well that explains everything," said Jarryd, rolling his eyes.

"I'm trying to drive," complained Brad. "Could you please sit still, Jarryd?"

"Still don't get it," Jarryd said sullenly, crossing his arms as he sat back.

"If it helps," said Kevin. "Kevin isn't my real name either." Jarryd just looked more puzzled but his questions were cut short when Brad pulled up outside St. John's. Jarryd climbed out the back seat, tugging his overloaded backpack out behind him. It was just a few blocks from there to the university and it wasn't long before Brad turned in to the Empire Road entrance

"Let's hope this works," said Brad as he pulled up to the boom at the gate. He'd gotten a notification on his student email that his parking access had been processed, but he'd been warned never to trust West bureaucracy. Stopping next to the card reader, Brad wound down his window with one hand and rummaged around in his glove compartment for his student card with the other.

Finding the card, Brad presented it at the card reader, only to suffer the drawn-out beep and red light of rejection. Brad tilted his head back in annoyance.

What do I do? he thought to himself, starting to panic a bit. It was almost time for the first lecture, so there were already three cars waiting behind him. Brad looked around frantically for a solution. He couldn't think of anything, so he just showed the card again. This time, the beep of rejection was accompanied by the sound of a car's horn, as someone behind him got impatient.

Sweet relief came when a passenger climbed out of one of the cars behind him, and approached the card reader, student card in hand.

"Jamie, this is getting to be a habit," said Tarryn.

"Brad," corrected Kevin.

"Hey," said Brad defensively, waving his student card for emphasis. "At least this one wasn't my fault." Tarryn presented her card at the reader, yielding the quick beep and green light of success.

"Wasn't it?" she asked, staring at his card. "Because your student card photo sure looks a lot like Kevin." Brad looked down at the glove box and saw his own student card sitting there in plain sight.

Brad stifled his embarrassment and forced a grin. Kevin twisted in his seat and unlocked the back door so Tarryn could climb in.

"I might as well head in with you, my boyfriend parks in postgrad and that's a bit out of my way," she said once she was inside.

Brad wasn't sure what part of what she said made him angry, but he tightened his grip on the steering wheel and clenched his jaw.

"Hey, this photo's pretty recent," Kevin commented. He had taken Tarryn's student card from her as she was climbing in, and was turning it over in his hands as he peered at it. "How long have you been at West?" he asked.

"Oh, I'm in third year," Tarryn replied. "But that photo is new. You have to get a new photo taken each year when you register, unless you can avoid it. Nathan's managed to keep the same photo for five years. They didn't require you to smile for it before 2007, so he's fought hard to avoid getting a new one."

Brad resolutely kept on driving while Kevin and Tarryn chatted.

"So Nathan has been here for five years?" Kevin asked.

"Oh yes," said Tarryn. "He's doing a Master's in Chemical Engineering, I think it is." Kevin nodded slowly, impressed, just as Brad approached the intersection, waiting for cross-traffic so he could make a right turn to go through the tunnel to West Campus.

"You said your boyfriend is doing postgrad, is he in Engineering as well?" asked Kevin, and Brad braked more abruptly than necessary.

"No," said Tarryn. "Master's in Computer Science. If you're interested, that's him driving past now." Tarryn waved as a VW Golf, much like Brad's, but a newer model, passed on their left.

*

Brad opened the door and walked in with Kevin. Tarryn had parted ways with them soon after they parked, going to her first lecture at eight o'clock.

Bernard was lying face down on a couch, snoring fitfully. Seth and James were crouched down next to the couch. They had assembled an assortment of small objects and were putting them into Bernard's hair. Seth raised a finger to his lips to signal Brad and Kevin to be quiet.

As Brad tiptoed across the room, he saw James shake his head and lay a restraining hand on Seth's shoulder. Seth's shoulders slumped. He lowered the wad of gum he was holding, and looked around for a piece of tissue paper to press it into. The only one he could find was already in Bernard's hair. He carefully retrieved it and wrapped it around his gum. Meanwhile, James was sprinkling lint into Bernard's sideburns.

As gently as he could, Brad wheeled an office chair up to the table, and pulled out his Criminal Law textbook.

He had just settled into reading when the club-room door swung open, and a guy in his mid-twenties strode in, carrying a cardboard box under one arm. He was about Brad's height, six feet. Lean but broad-shouldered, his straight back was a sharp contrast with WARP's contagious slouch. He wore a maroon t-shirt with his faded black jeans, rather than the blue jeans and black t-shirt that seemed to be an unspoken dress code in WARP. He had wavy brown hair and deep blue eyes.

Seth winced as the swinging door hit the wall, and held his breath as he looked at Bernard to see if he'd wake. The newcomer raised an eyebrow and tilted his head sideways in question.

Seth once again raised a finger to his lips to signal quiet and James carefully got to his feet, padding across the room.

"Hey Evan," whispered James. "What's in the box?" he continued, nodding toward the box that Evan was carrying. Evan grinned mischievously, and turned the box around to show off the label.

'Christmas tree stuff' the label read.

"Good time to bring this stuff back for James," said Evan, placing the box on the table and nodding towards Bernard's sleeping form. "Dig in guys, I'm feeling festive."

With a wicked grin, James pulled out a handful of silver tinsel. Kevin picked out a fluffy Santa doll. Brad reached in and grabbed a shiny silver bell. Before he could stop himself, he rang it.

Bernard snorted in response to the noise, placing a hand on the back of the couch to drag himself into a sitting position with a groan. Seth covered his eyes with the palm of his hand. Kevin shook his head sadly. Bernard was staring suspiciously at a raisin he'd pulled out of his beard.

"Brad, hold still while I shove that bell down your throat," said James, advancing on Brad.

"Give the kid a break," Evan said to James. "You were just as bad when you were a first-year. Remember the time you called the cops on Nathan?" James looked down at his feet and shrugged. "And Seth," Evan continued. "Remember the time YOU called the cops on Nathan?" Seth lowered his eyes as well.

With a shrug, Bernard popped the raisin into his mouth and chewed contemplatively. Evan turned to Kevin and Brad with a grin.

"So what are we calling you two?" Evan asked.

"Kevin," replied Kevin. "And the genius with the bell is Brad."

"Nice to meet you guys. As you heard, I'm Evan," said Evan. "I'll just leave this here in the club-room," he continued, putting the box down on the table. "We'll get a chance to decorate Bernard some other time."

Hearing his name, Bernard looked across the room.

"Some party last night, huh Evan?" said Bernard, rubbing his eyes of sleep, after two attempts to locate them.

"It was indeed," said Evan. "I assume you slept here," he continued, an expression of distaste on his face.

"Well, yeah. I could hardly drive in that state," said Bernard. "Hell, I barely made it to the club-room." As Bernard said this, the club-room door was opened again, and Tarryn walked in. She crossed the room to where Evan was standing and hugged him.

Brad's eyes widened in surprise and he glared in Evan's direction.

"Hey," said Bernard. "You know the rules, no couple stuff in the club-room."

"That from the guy who's been bringing Tara here after hours?" said Tarryn.

"My house is really far," grumbled Bernard, looking sheepish.

"Wait, what?" demanded James. "I won't have your inbred DNA all over the couches, not while I'm president. Bernard, hand over your club-room key. Now."

Chapter 5

Jamie "Bradford" Rogers: The life of a university student, the excitement never stops!
27 April, 2010

*

Brad rounded the corner in the corridor, flanked by Kevin, only to see a small group sitting disconsolately outside WARP's door.

Bernard was sitting with his back against the wall and his legs splayed. He was in conversation with a petite blonde girl who was sitting across from him, arms wrapped around her knees. She looked flushed and angry, and Brad could hear her voice from the end of the corridor.

"Try calling James again. If I don't get my notebook out of that room before this tut, I swear I'll tell the Students' council what you did with the club budget."

With a resigned sigh, Bernard leaned over to hit redial on his cellphone, which was lying on the ground next to him.

"You have reached the voice mailbox of James Green. Leave a message after the tone. Anything you say can and will be used against you."

"Hey Brad, Kevin," said Bernard by way of greeting. "This is Lauren. Lauren, these are Brad and Kevin. They're filthy first-years, like you. Possibly filthier." Brad extended a hand, which Lauren ignored. She was pretty in a generic way. Long blonde hair, pale complexion, good cheekbones.

"Try calling Nathan," suggested Lauren. "He has a club-room key." Bernard sighed and rubbed his temples. He looked like he was getting a headache. Once again, he dialled a number and put his phone down next to him.

"Hello?" came the answer over speaker phone. The voice was male, but didn't sound like Nathan. Bernard paused, confused. "Can I help you?" the speaker continued.

"This is Bernard. I'm looking for Nathan?" asked Bernard.

"This is Ari." said the voice on the other side. "Bernard, how did you get my number?"

"No idea dude, had it under Nathan's name," Bernard replied. "I think I got it from him."

"Weird," said Ari, hanging up. Lauren sighed in frustration and put her head down on her arms.

"Take a seat, guys," said Bernard, waving at the floor next to him. "Looks like we're stuck here until Seth finishes his test."

Brad thought for a moment about heading to a library. Instead, he folded his legs and reached into his bag for his Customary Law textbook. As he rummaged around his hand bumped into his 3DS. He never had gotten around to finishing Pokemon Diamond, and that Customary Law tut was only at 2pm. He could afford some time off.

"Well, I'm out of time" said Lauren a few minutes later, standing up. "I guess I'll just go fail English."

"Bye then," said Bernard, staring disconsolately after her as she left.

"So," said Kevin, filling the awkward silence. "Who's Ari?"

"I suppose you'd say he's a friend of Nathan's, insofar as that term is appropriate. They were in the same class through undergrad and they're doing Master's degrees under the same supervisors."

Bernard was interrupted by the sound of footsteps echoing along the corner. Evan rounded the corner, followed by James, awkwardly trying to match Evan's long stride.

"Where were you guys?" demanded Bernard, pointing angrily at the locked gate. "If you aren't gonna be available to open up the room, you should just give me back my key."

"Over Tara's dead body," said James levelly. "And it just so happens," he continued, drawing himself up with offended dignity. "We were queuing at Rosebank to reserve tickets for the Iron Man 2 advance screening. Which is in like an hour, so let's get going. Bernard, you can't come anymore. We'll take Kevin instead, he doesn't argue with me."

"Where's Seth?" said Evan, looking around. "I figured he'd be coming with."

"He's writing a test," said Bernard.

"Forget Seth!" said James. "Seth was weak. We'll take Kevin instead."

"We're already taking Kevin," said Evan.

"Right, right," said James. "Spare seat for Bernard's snacks, then. Or we can scalp it at the venue. Kevin, Evan, let's get going."

James turned on his heel and strode down the corridor.

"We reserved six tickets," said Evan, after James was out of earshot. "You guys might as well come along too. Bernard, you ride with Seth. He's meeting us there, he'll be done with his test pretty soon."

*

"So who's Tara?" Brad asked as he pulled on his seatbelt. He was in the back seat of Evan's car, next to Kevin. "Is she Bernard's girlfriend or something?"

"Something like that," replied James from the front passenger seat. "I thought you'd met her actually, she was at the WARP party the other day. Kevin definitely met her. If he hadn't left early, he'd be where Bernard is, and Bernard would still be single, the way he should be."

"I wasn't invited to any party," Brad complained, furrowing his eyebrows. "What's the deal?"

"I found a Brad on the club mailing list, it was one of the first invites I sent out," protested James. "It's not my fault if you don't read your email."

"James," said Evan. "His real name isn't Brad."

"So who did I invite?" said James.

"I think it was that sweaty guy, the one from Kevin's high-school," said Evan. "He said his name was Brad." Kevin nodded to confirm this.

"Hydrant?" asked James, incredulous. "I can't believe I invited that guy instead of Brad. What if he likes the club and comes again? What if he never discovers showering?"

"Relax," said Evan. "Nathan made him cry, I don't think we'll be seeing him again."

"Were those really tears, though?" asked James. "Or was he just sweating from his eyeballs too?"

Brad was about to get the conversation back on track and find out who Tara was, but just as he was framing his question in his head, Evan pulled into the underground parking at Rosebank shopping centre.

"To the Prestige Cinema!" James announced grandly, opening his door even before the car had stopped completely.

*

When they arrived at the cinema foyer the blood drained from Evan's face, and his fists tightened. He grabbed James's shoulder, bringing him to an abrupt halt, just as he approached the ticket counter.

"We're watching something else," said Evan.

"No. Why?" asked James, confused. "We came here specifically to watch Iron Man 2. We queued for two hours this morning specifically to reserve tickets for Iron Man 2. Not to mention, the other movies are all garbage."

"Dude, *she* just picked up a ticket for Iron Man 2. And she asked for front row. We're in the front row. We'll be sitting next to her."

"Uh, who are you talking about?" asked Brad, just as Evan leapt behind him, to hide from a girl who turned in their direction as she walked away from the counter.

"Did she see me?" asked Evan. "She didn't see me, right?"

"She didn't see you," James reassured him. "At least, not until I pointed at you and waved." Shocked, Evan peeked out from behind Brad, right into the eyes of the girl in question. He shot a look of betrayal at James.

"Look," said James. "You can block people on Facebook, but not in real life. So make nice," he finished, making shooing motions with his hands.

"You don't understand," said Evan. "She's not just my ex's sister, she's also my ex."

"If you're going to hide behind one of your friends," she said, wearily. "At least pick Bernard so that you aren't completely visible."

"Oh, a fat joke," said Evan. "How mature."

"At least I'm capable of being an adult about this," she said, rolling her eyes. "If you can't handle me being around I'll go watch something else," she finished, handing over her ticket.

"What was that about?" Brad asked as she walked away.

"Don't worry about it," said James, waving away the question. "If we can scalp this ticket, then she just paid for our snacks."

"Scalping tickets is illegal," said Brad reproachfully.

"And who is this 'we'?" added Evan, clutching the extra ticket possessively.

*

Bernard Cronje: Iron Man 2 advance screening: R80. Snacks and drinks: snuck in under my jacket. Seeing Evan thrown out by security: priceless.
12 May, 2010

Chapter 6

Nathan Hillary: Horror movies teach us one thing; the early bird dies.
18 May, 2010

*

Brad glared blearily at his alarm clock. Just out of arm's reach, it wailed at him insistently. Shuffling across his room with his duvet wrapped around him for warmth, Brad silenced his tormentor and pulled open his curtains.

The front lawn was covered in pristine white frost, the first of the season. Jamie watched as Jarryd darted toward the front gate, hunched against the cold and leaving footprints of crushed frost behind him. Jarryd back-pedalled desperately, putting out a hand to stop himself as he skidded toward the gate. Stopping just short of impact, Jarryd grabbed the newspaper and charged back to the front door.

"And don't slam the door!" came the sound of Mrs Rogers's voice from downstairs, accompanied by the sound of the front door slamming shut. Brad winced as his door was pulled open by Jarryd, letting in a chilly draft.

"Morning fatty," said Jarryd with an impish grin. "Put some pants on, breakfast's getting cold!" he continued, rushing back out of Brad's room with a characteristic clatter.

"Damnit Jarryd, do you hate doors or something?" demanded Brad, brushing flecks of ceiling paint from his hair as his younger brother ran back down the passage.

Brad glanced down at his clock and his eyebrows lifted in surprise. He was running late. Stuffing an armful of clothes under his arm, Brad gripped his duvet tightly and shuffled to the bathroom to shower.

*

"You're late," said Kevin as he climbed into Brad's car. "And where's Jarryd?"

"My mom had to take him in. I overslept," answered Brad. "What's in the bag?" he asked, gesturing at a drawstring cloth bag that Kevin was carrying.

"Dice," answered Kevin, giving the bag a quick shake.

"Dice?" asked Brad, puzzled.

"You know, dice?" said Kevin, grinning. "Multi-sided things, bunch of numbers on them?"

"I know what dice are," said Brad. "I wanted to know why you have a bag of them."

"Apparently I need them for role-playing," explained Kevin.

"What, like Dungeons and Dragons?" asked Brad.

"I thank you for making that assumption. This particular version is Star Wars themed." At mention of Star Wars, Brad's ears pricked up.

"So when is this happening?" asked Brad.

"Bernard runs a game in the club-room on Tuesday mornings," said Kevin. "First session of the campaign is today, you should totally join in."

"I'm free-ish on Tuesday mornings," replied Brad. "I'll come take a look."

*

By mid-morning, a diverse group had gathered in the club-room for Bernard's campaign. Joining Brad and Kevin was Nathan's colleague Ari, who turned out to be a stocky Greek with an unruly mop of thick black hair. The fourth member of the group was Matt, an older guy with a tremulous voice and a slight stoop to his posture. The four of them were seated around the central table in the WARP clubroom, waiting for Bernard to get back from the bathroom so they could get started.

"Any of you have any idea how to play?" asked Ari, leaning over the table and peering dubiously at a rulebook. Brad glanced at Kevin, and they both shook their heads.

"Nathan explained it a little bit, when he recruited me," answered Matt. "I'm Matt, by the way. This Star Wars system is basically the same as standard DnD."

"Yes," said Kevin. "But what do we actually do?"

"Well, you roll your attack against the enemy's Reflex, Will or Fortitude defense."

"So no saving throws?" asked Ari.

"No saving throws," replied Matt.

"Ok cool, no saving throws," said Kevin. "But what do we actually do?"

"Bernard's campaigns are normally pretty basic dungeon crawls, nothing complex," said Matt, shrugging.

"But," said Kevin, very slowly. "What do we actually do?"

Matt's lesson was interrupted as Bernard walked into the room, wringing his hands and grinning.

"Fresh meat," he said, eyeing them and chuckling. "You gentlemen will be setting out from the Mos Eisley cantina, the galaxy's most wretched hive of scum and villainy." Bernard handed blank character sheets around the table. "You'll start off at level 1 to get a feel for the system. I'm restricting you to the core rulebook for this campaign, no exceptions."

Ari leafed through the rulebook in front of him on the table, occasionally jotting something down on his character sheet. Matt rifled through his backpack, eventually producing a completed character sheet, which he handed to Bernard.

"I already made my character at home," explained Matt. Bernard glanced at the sheet and grimaced.

"Urgh, you're playing a Human Noble? Boring. Otherwise, everything checks out. Maybe change the name, 'William Wetwiper' isn't very Star-Wars-y." Confused, Brad stuck his hand up to ask questions. Ari, meanwhile, had finished up his own character sheet and handed it to Bernard for checking.

"A Wookie Scoundrel, named Aaaarrri? I like it!" said Bernard, glancing over the sheet. "But your attack modifier is wrong. Add your dexterity modifier to your level." Bernard finally noticed that Brad had his hand up. "You aren't in class Brad, you can just ask questions."

"In that case," said Brad. "What do we actually do?"

"It's simple," said Bernard. "Well, simple-ish." He reached over and took Brad's character sheet from him to demonstrate on. "Every time you try and do something, be it pick up a heavy rock or shoot someone in combat, you roll a d20 and add an appropriate modifier, and that determines how successful you are. How high that total has to be depends on how difficult what you're doing is. Let's say it's a pretty big rock, we might give it a challenge rating of 20. If your strength modifier is 5, then you would have to roll a 15 to successfully pick it up. When you attack someone, you do the same with your attack and their defense. It even works with trying to do stuff in conversation. If you're trying to persuade someone of something, then depending how you're doing it you use your bluff check or your diplomacy or whatever."

"And how does levelling work?" asked Brad, nodding slowly.

"As you gain levels you get ability points to assign, and those then change your modifiers making your character better at certain things. You also get to pick skills, which do more specific stuff. That includes special attacks and whatnot."

"And damage?" asked Brad. "How does that work?"

"Each character has a certain number of hit-points and doing damage removes them. Get down to zero and you die, basically. Unless you get revived, but we'll deal with that when we come to it."

"That all makes sense," said Kevin. "But what do we actually do?"

"I describe your environment to you," said Bernard. "And you decide what you want to do in it. Like where to go, and who to talk to and things like that. And of course, who to fight." He handed back Brad's character sheet. "The first step is to choose your class and your species. Different classes have access to different skills, and different species have various bonuses and penalties." Brad had already stopped listening and written 'Human Jedi' on the sheet.

*

Chapter 7

Jamie "Bradford" Rogers: "Midterms did not go as well as I'd hoped. I'll need to buckle down, or I'll be repeating some subjects next year"
 26 July, 2010
  2 comments: **Bernard Cronje:** "Don't worry Brad, it happens to the best of us."
   Nathan Hillary: "No. It doesn't."

*

"Who's hogging the wi-fi?" Bernard demanded, looking up from his laptop. "Seth, are you downloading aircraft maintenance manuals again?"

It was a cold winter morning and Brad was skipping class to enjoy the cosy warmth of the club-room's heaters. Evan was relaxing on the couch across from him while Bernard and Seth were engrossed in their respective laptops and Kevin was reading through a textbook at the table.

"Actually it's the first episode of Sherlock," Seth replied, pointing at his own laptop. "The manuals go on my tablet for easy reading," he added, surreptitiously placing his jacket over that selfsame tablet.

"Well, I can't play DOTA with this much lag," said Bernard, snapping his laptop shut. "I died like twenty times in that game."

"So what you're saying," said Seth. "Is that the lag stops you from dying as much as you normally do?" Before Bernard could come up with a clever retort, so somewhere in the span of two to five minutes later, there was a knock at the door.

"Come in!" said Kevin, and the door opened slightly. A head poked in, with a mop of dark hair.

"Is this the WARP club room?" asked the newcomer leaning in through the doorway.

"This is WARP," said Kevin. "Are you coming in?"

"I'll be back in a couple of minutes," came the reply. "I just need to fetch my friend. We've been looking for this place since O-Week." With that, the newcomer darted back out of the room, closing the door behind him.

"He seemed nice," said Kevin. "And we could use some new blood."

"I have a better idea," said Evan. "Well, funnier, at least. How about he comes back to find us all exactly where we were, just without pants?"

"I'm on board," said Bernard, lobbing his jeans over Brad's head to land out of sight behind the couch.

"You owe me for this," added Seth, carefully folding his jeans and sliding them under his bag.

"What the hell, guys?" demanded Brad, shocked. "This is a bad idea."

"Bad idea?" said Evan, depositing his own jeans behind the couch. "Let's see how bad."

Brad looked around the room at the expectant faces of his barelegged friends.

"One of us. One of us," chanted Kevin, dropping his jeans behind the couch and darting back to his seat.

"Fine," said Brad, reaching a decision. "But I'll need some help getting these over my shoes." It took a strong pull from Evan and Bernard but in mere moments, Brad was back on the couch feeling more grateful than ever that the club-room was heated in the winter. He willed himself to hold a straight face as he heard voices approaching from the corridor outside.

"Yeah, this one here," said the guy they'd seen earlier. "These guys seem pretty cool." With that, the door opened and he stepped in along with his friend.

"Hello again," said Evan brightly. "You didn't mention that your friend is a girl."

*

Bernard Cronje: One inch to the left and this hole in my boxers would be a felony.
26 July, 2010

*

"Do you mind waiting a bit before we head home?" Kevin asked.

"Yeah, no problem," Brad replied. "What's up?"

"Well," said Kevin. "I realised today that my legs could do with some beefing up, so I want to go to Sports Admin and maybe sign up for a sport."

"I guess I could do the same," said Brad, having a flashback to that morning's incident. "What sport do you have in mind?"

"I'll figure it out when I get there," said Kevin, shrugging.

"Fair enough," said Brad. "Let's get going."

*

"What's with this queue?" asked Brad when they reached the Sports Admin office. "Surely there aren't this many people signing up for sports clubs at this time of year?"

"Signing up?" said the guy ahead of them in the queue. "I'm deregistering. I joined the volleyball club expecting some fun and a bit of exercise, but it turns out they literally don't even own a volleyball."

"Same with me," said someone from further ahead in the queue. "I'm ditching rowing. All they do is run a bar on Thursday nights, and you don't even have to be a member to drink there."

"Athletics is the same," said someone else. "Except their bar opens on Wednesdays."

"I am beginning to reconsider," said Kevin. As he turned to leave the queue, he almost bumped into Bernard.

"You boys gonna keep me company while I drop out of fencing?" said Bernard. "This queue looks pretty rough."

"Are you also deregistering because the club doesn't do anything?" Kevin asked.

"What? No, I love the club." said Bernard. "I've been kicked out. One little accidental stabbing and they freak out. This university is turning into a nanny state."

"Accidental stabbing sounds pretty serious," said Kevin. "How did that happen with all that protective gear?"

"Protective...what?" said Bernard, confused. "No, no. It happened at the bar. And she'll be alright, eventually."

Chapter 8

Jamie "Bradford" Rogers: Spring is finally here! Time for blue skies, warm sun and flip-flops! And year-end assignments, of course.
    1 September, 2010
    1 comment: **James Green:** More like time for the Engineer's breakfast. Bacon, beer and pancakes out on the Amic Deck.

*

"Why does this suck?" James lamented. "There can't possibly be this many first-years in engineering, how is it this crowded?"

"I don't get it," said Brad. "None of us are engineers anyway. If we're here why wouldn't everyone else be as well?"

"Well yes but that's not how it works," said James, who glanced down at his beer as if wondering how it had gotten so empty. "Engineers' breakfast was a thing arranged by older engineering students, and they'd invite their friends and stuff. So once you'd been at West for a while, you'd be in the loop. WARP was mostly engineers back in the day so it was a big thing for us. Now it's millions of first-years being retarded."

The breakfast was taking place in a parking lot on the far corner of West Campus, far from any buildings Brad was familiar with. Brad was standing with the rest of WARP, sipping beer while bacon sizzled on Evan's portable grill. The conversation stopped in breathless silence as Bernard flipped a pancake. Pieces of his first attempt were still dangling from his beard. When the pancake landed neatly back in the pan, Bernard grinned triumphantly and flashed a thumbs-up to the rest of the group.

"It's not so bad," said Evan, patting James on the shoulder. "Yeah, this parking lot doesn't have a view like the Amic deck, but at least it's out of the wind."

"Not so bad?" demanded James, incredulous. "There's a pair of guys at the ambulance because they tried to arm-wrestle on a hot stove-top. And why do these first-years all think it's acceptable to wander around shirtless?"

"They don't really understand that they aren't in high-school anymore," Seth speculated. "Take that dumbass over there with the giant sunglasses. In high-school, that blurry pair of abs would move him a notch up the social ladder. Here, he just looks like a douchebag."

Brad mentally filed this information away. *No social ladder. Don't need abs.*

"What you aren't thinking about," said Evan. "Is just how low that sets the bar. Typically, women have an extensive mental checklist when picking guys, but today they'll be like 'Gee, that guy hardly puked on me at all, I should probably marry him. And find out his name.' In that order." As if to punctuate Evan's point, a loud slap rang out. "Take that guy as an example," Evan added without looking in the direction of the slap. "He just covered that girl in Black Label and half-digested pancake, but he still reckons he's in with a shot. And you know what? If he can get her a towel before anyone else, he is."

As he finished saying this, Evan opened his cooler box and pulled a towel out from it, passing it into Bernard's waiting hands.

"Now Bernard," said James. "Try not to puke on her again."

Brad sipped at his beer, feeling awkward. He didn't really like beer, and he was a bit out of place at this breakfast.

"Where's the nearest bathroom?" he asked the group in general. An innocuous question, or so Brad thought, but it drew a flurry of activity from the rest of the group.

Evan pulled a sheet of paper from his backpack and unfolded it to peer at it in midair. James took a pristine sheet of laminated board from his own backpack, and Seth had flipped open his laptop and was punching keys.

"I have no data for this region," said Seth, to Brad's confusion.

"All I've got nearby are the bathrooms by the basketball courts, and they're pretty bad. Emergencies only," said Evan.

James shrugged. "Closest I've got are in the Commerce Building, and that's a ten minute walk from here," he said.

"Are those...maps?" asked Brad, puzzled. "With bathrooms marked on them?"

"Well yes," replied James. "Bernard's has bushes too. He says it saves water but he's actually just lazy."

"None of you could tell me where to find a library," asked Brad, disbelieving. "But you're telling me that you guys have maps to all the campus bathrooms?"

"Well yeah," said Evan. "Don't you have a bathroom map yet?"

"I mostly just use the ones in the Matrix," replied Brad. "The ones downstairs from the clubroom." The group turned to Brad, staring in horror.

Feeling embarrassed and defensive, Brad just shrugged.

"I went into the Matrix bathrooms one time when I was a first year," said Evan. "And I swear to God, my bladder emptied back into my bloodstream."

"That bathroom is the sole reason the Medical School moved onto a separate campus," added James.

"Most bathrooms on West are dirty enough to start a zombie outbreak," said Seth. "The matrix bathrooms are on a whole other level. They could stop one."

"Okay I get it," said Brad, defensively. "So what bathrooms should I use?"

"Dude, no-one's going to just tell you where the best bathrooms are," explained James. "You keep good bathrooms secret, that's how they stay good. The fewer people know about a bathroom the less it gets used."

"It's true," added Evan. "The key to good hygiene is secrecy. The best bathrooms aren't even labelled as bathrooms."

*

'Emergencies only' was what Evan had said about the basketball court bathrooms. Brad could only agree, but by the time he reached them the situation had become an emergency. Brad had glimpsed these basketball courts from Empire Road when driving past West, but he'd never noticed the tiny outhouse with its crumbling brickwork and rusted iron roof.

Walking through the door, Brad stopped for a moment to let his eyes adjust to the dark. Brad got to it as soon as he could see well enough to do what he needed to, anxious to get out before his eyes adjusted all the way. A stringent chemical smell and faint scuttling noises led him to suspect there were things he was better off not seeing.

Squinting in the bright sunlight, Brad used the water bottle from his back pack to wash his hands. After rubbing his hands dry on his jeans, he walked a little way away from the smell that was following him out of the bathroom and sat down on the grass. He still had his campus map from orientation week, and he drew a neat cross on it to mark the bathroom he had just used.

Brad thought briefly about heading back to the breakfast, but decided against it. Shirtless douchebags having vomiting contests wasn't his idea of a good time. He had no classes that morning, and of course the club-room was empty because everyone was at the breakfast. Brad resolved to do some legwork and add to his bathroom map.

*

Brad's search started with the Umthombo building, right next to the Matrix, in front of the library lawns. Since he spent so much time at the Matrix it made sense to find bathrooms nearby. Plenty of people had the same idea, unfortunately, judging by the state of the ground floor bathrooms at Umthombo. There was a slightly cleaner set of bathrooms on the first floor, but only slightly cleaner. Decent in a pinch.

Brad remembered what Evan had mentioned at the breakfast; the best bathrooms weren't labelled as such. So Brad started just checking every door that wasn't labelled as a lecture venue. He saw terrible things.

Brad's next stop was the Wartenweiler library. It was the next building along after Umthombo, up a flight of stairs and at the far end of the lawns. Like all libraries at West, it had an access turnstile and required a student card to swipe to get in. Clean and quiet, the library building held promise. Brad followed the signs and climbed a flight of stairs to the bathrooms. *You have to swipe in AND climb stairs?* Brad thought. *Big deterrents, I bet these bathrooms hardly get used.*

As Brad walked into the bathrooms, he smiled broadly. Not only were they totally empty, they were also the cleanest he had seen on campus. Brad made a note on his map and made to leave. A quick jog down the stairs and Brad presented his student card at the turnstile only to hear the harsh bleep of rejection, made even more jarring by the quiet of the library lobby. Hesitantly, Brad tried it again and winced when he got the same result.

Brad furrowed his brow in thought. Something tickled his memory but he couldn't quite call it to mind. Not knowing what to do, Brad sent Kevin a text: 'Hey Kevin, I went into the library but now my card won't let me out. Could you maybe swipe me out with your card, I don't know what's happening.' Kevin's reply came moments later.

'w8 15 mins try agn, turnstiles hav delay thingy'

Brad put his palm to his head as the memory slotted back into place. During one of the few o-week lectures he had attended he'd been told that access turnstiles had a fifteen minute delay after one swipe before they'd allow access again.

Brad took out his map and made a notation: 'long wait; #2 only'.

*

Chapter 9

Nathan Hillary: Procrastination. Because every problem deserves a chance to solve itself
      6 December 2010

*

Brad scowled at the gap between his curtains. The arrival of Spring had its downsides, including bright sunlight long before Brad wanted to be awake. Still in his pyjamas, he made his way downstairs to the kitchen.

His mother greeted him with a bright smile. Brad tried to return a smile of his own but with his eyes still half-closed the result was far from friendly-looking.

"Oh dear," said Brad's mom. "Looks like someone's having a rough morning. Can I pour you some orange juice?"

"Only if orange juice is code for a stronger version of coffee," replied Brad, rubbing his eyes. He'd been up late with his Player's Handbook, optimizing his skill choices for Bernard's Star Wars campaign.

Brad stared vacantly at the coffee machine as it filled his cup. When it was about halfway he winced at the grating sound of his alarm going off upstairs in his room.

"Jamie, would you go turn that thing off?" his mom asked, exasperated.

"I'll get it!" yelled Jarryd from upstairs. "Fatty struggles with the stairs!" Brad felt more grateful to be settling down with his coffee than he was angry about the comment.

"Are you sleeping alright, dear?" Brad's mom asked, concerned. Brad shrugged.

"I've just got a lot of work. Exams coming up and all."

"So you aren't up all night texting some girl, then?" his mom said with a knowing smile. "Not that I'd be angry if that's the problem. You just need to learn to manage your time so you get a good night's rest."

Brad stared morosely at his empty coffee mug as he tried to summon the energy to get up and pour himself another. Exam marks had been released the night before. Brad had failed, and he wasn't looking forward to breaking that news to his parents.

Brad had always been the kind of guy to try games on Easy Mode first, so he was waiting for his mom to go to work so he could tackle his dad.

After about ten minutes of waiting, Elliot Rogers walked into the kitchen with a bag of groceries in each hand.

"Grab some health-food boxes out the cupboard, would you?" Elliot asked. "I need to hide some snacks from Jarryd."

"Don't want him eating all the good stuff, huh?" Brad asked, rummaging in the cupboard where the low-GI food was kept.

"Exactly," said Elliot. "Now pass me something wholegrain so I can stash these cookies."

Brad obliged, handing his father an empty box of All-Bran.

"Listen Dad," said Brad. "There's something I need to talk about." His dad put down what he was doing and turned to face him directly. "It's about my exams," Brad began.

"Listen," his dad said. "I think I know where this is going and failing a few subjects is nothing to be embarrassed about."

"Really?" said Brad, surprise overwhelming his relief. "I thought you were very keen on academics."

"Well that's the official story," Brad's dad said, a mischievous grin crinkling the laugh lines around his eyes. "I'm a Deputy Headmaster, after all. But," he continued. "I wasn't quite so focused back when I was your age. Take a seat," he added, doing so himself. "And I'll tell you about my university career. Education wasn't my first choice of degree," Elliot explained once Brad was sitting across from him. "I tried Engineering first, but that was a disaster. Plan B was Actuarial Science, which went a little better. I passed an entire two subjects there, but it turned out both of them were credits I could transfer to teaching. And that's how I chose my career."

Brad shifted in his chair. All his life, his dad had been utterly dependable and in control. Brad couldn't imagine him failing at anything.

"There are just so many distractions at that age," Elliot continued. "And back then, we didn't even have TV or Internet. Honestly I'd have been surprised if you had passed. This is your first time going to class with girls, after all."

"That's reassuring to hear," said Brad, absentmindedly grabbing a handful of chips from a broccoli packet. "But I'm still a bit nervous about telling mom."

"I guess I can take care of that," said Elliot. "I've had decades of practice explaining things to her."

"Thanks dad," said Brad.

"Jarryd's your problem, though," said Elliot.

Chapter 10

Nathan Hillary: Humility is a crutch for those who lack talent
      17 January 2011

*

"If you'd just made it into second-year, you wouldn't have to go to O-week," said Jarryd, grinning insolently. Brad exhaled heavily.

"Jarryd, that's got nothing to do with it. I'm going to O-week to recruit for WARP. And I am mostly in second year. It's just Customary Law that I'm repeating."

It was just after dawn and Brad was sitting in the kitchen, finishing his coffee while Jarryd pestered him. All WARP regulars were required to help out by taking shifts at the recruiting stall during O-week and Brad had been assigned the early morning shift every day that week. Monday would see him working with Nathan.

"You should sign up for the campus gym while you're there," suggested Jarryd. "You've gotten even fatter since you became a geek."

"Thanks Jarryd, real nice of you to say," said Brad, getting up from the table. "But I have to get going, Nathan will be waiting for me."

'Nathan's been our most successful recruiter for five years running,' James's email had said. 'So he's the best bet for teaching noobs how to do it. That's why you're paired with him. To learn.'

Brad was full of curiosity; he could hardly imagine Nathan being nice to someone long enough to get them to join the club.

*

"Don't be nice to people," was Nathan's first piece of advice. "It's easy to ignore someone who's being nice to you." He had his feet up on the table and was explaining his methods to Brad while they waited for the crowds to arrive. "You need to engage people, get them interested. Just rattling off a list of what WARP does will get you nowhere. Anyone who really cares about that would join anyway, and people hear a dozen standardised sales pitches just walking through this tent. You need to stand out. Here, try this girl."

As he said this last, Nathan pointed discreetly at a wide-eyed first year walking past with an armful of textbooks and a dazed expression.

"Excuse me," said Brad politely. "Can I interest you in joining our club?" She ignored him, and walked on by. Nathan face-palmed.

"Yeah, Brad, sure. I bet she hasn't heard the words 'excuse me' a hundred times today. Like I said, you have to break past the desensitisation. Observe." Nathan pointed at another girl on her way past.

"If I told you that you have a wonderful body," Nathan began. The first-year rolled her eyes and sighed, barely breaking stride. "Would you realise I'm lying?" Nathan finished. The girl gasped, and Nathan flashed a mischievous grin as she glared at him.

"So are you like the Big Bang Theory guys?" she asked as she walked up to the stall. Tall and leggy, she had long auburn hair and bright green eyes.

"Pretty much," said Nathan. "We just don't have a hot girl. Otherwise, we're identical."

"Well, you have one now," she said, reaching for a form.

"Eh," said Nathan as she signed. "We can do better."

"At least I'm better looking than the guys in the club," she said with a smile.

"Present company excluded, of course," added Nathan.

"Present company emphasised," she corrected as she walked away with a distinct sway of the hips.

"Keep walking like that!" Nathan yelled after her. "It burns calories."

"I can't believe that actually worked," said Brad, staring at her signup sheet. 'Claudia O'Reilly', it said. A psychology student, and a first year based on the student number.

"It often doesn't," Nathan said, shrugging. "But it gets their attention, and then you have a chance. This is a numbers game." He grimaced. "Oh, and get used to people asking about Big Bang Theory, it'll happen a lot. That show has made geeks into circus animals; people expect us to entertain them. This dude here even brought popcorn." Brad looked up and there was indeed a guy walking past stalls eating from a box of popcorn.

"You. Yeah, you!" Nathan said to him. "You look like a guy with a really girly signature."

"I do not!" he protested.

"Oh yes?" said Nathan, sliding a form toward the guy and proffering a pen. "Prove it." With a raised eyebrow, the guy walked up to the stall.

"So what's this club all about?" he asked. He was Indian. Slightly below average height, he wore baggy jeans and a faded t-shirt.

"I have no idea," replied Nathan. "They hire me for O-week because they can't communicate with humans. Brad, tell this guy what WARP's about."

"Uh..." said Brad, panicking slightly. "We mostly just sort of hang out in the club-room. Sometimes we play games and stuff. And we have couches. I'm Brad by the way," he finished.

"I'm Melvyn, and that sounds amazing. Sign me up."

"Congrats Brad, your first recruitment," said Nathan, without much enthusiasm.

"Yeah, way to go Brad," said Melvyn, flashing an enthusiastic thumbs up. "Nice work." Brad looked at him strangely.

"He'll fit in just fine," said Nathan. "Melvyn, take a seat and help Brad recruit. I'm gonna head off and get coffee."

With a triumphant grin, Melvyn settled down behind the table, taking Nathan's seat.

"So how do we do this?" Melvyn asked through a mouthful of popcorn.

"As far as I can gather we insult people and somehow that makes them sign up," explained Brad. Melvyn looked at him dubiously.

"If you say so, man. I've only been here for thirty seconds. I guess I'll take your word for it." Eager to get started and do his bit for WARP, Brad peered down the aisle, looking for a likely target.

"Hey! Yeah, you. Where'd you get those shoes?" Brad made a promising start. "If I were you, I uh...wouldn't have gotten them," he finished.

"Burn!" yelled Melvin, supportively. The guy Brad had addressed turned in his direction with a confused look.

"Buddy, you have the same shoes," he said. "Mine are just cleaner," he finished, walking away and shaking his head. Melvyn patted Brad on the shoulder consolingly.

"You'll get the hang of it," he said. "Try this lady here, she looks promising." Brad scanned her up and down, zeroing in on the best angle of attack.

"Hey lady," he said. "Aren't you a bit old to be a student?" he finished with a triumphant smile. She stopped and looked closely at Brad's face.

"Aren't you repeating my Customary Law class?" she said pointedly. "You'll do better this year if you actually attend lectures," she added. Brad panicked and just pretended to be reading something on his phone until she eventually left.

"Almost had her," said Melvyn encouragingly. "Here, let me have a go. Hey you," he said to another passer-by. "Aren't you a little young to be in university?"

"Mom!" the boy yelled, and his mother clutched him protectively as she hurried away from the stall.

"Brad," said a voice from the side of the stall. "What the hell are you doing?" It was James, standing and watching with an incredulous look on his face. "And who is this guy?" he finished, pointing at Melvyn.

*

Melvyn's early misfires failed to deter him and he decided to stick around the stall even after James and Bernard arrived to take over. Brad, on the other hand, started making his way to the club-room to take a break. On his way he was stopped by the sound of a familiar voice.

"Jamie!" it was Tarryn, walking the other way, along with Lauren, the blonde that Brad had seen around WARP a few times. "So nice to see you," Tarryn continued. Brad awkwardly manoeuvred his arms around her as she gave him a friendly hug. "How was your first taste of recruiting?" Tarryn asked.

"Up and down," said Brad with a shrug. "Did you two just come from the club-room?" he asked.

"We did," said Tarryn. "Evan's up there with Kevin and Seth, playing Guitar Hero instead of recruiting." Brad brightened up at the mention of Guitar Hero. He'd been practicing all holiday and he liked the idea of beating Evan at something. "So we're off to do our bit," Tarryn continued. "It's best if some girls run the stall from time to time."

"She promised me lunch if I helped," added Lauren.

"So who's down at the stall right now?" Tarryn asked.

"James and Bernard are there with Melvyn," Brad answered absentmindedly. "So which Guitar Hero are they playing?"

"I didn't even know there were different ones until this morning," said Tarryn. *Probably Guitar Hero 6* thought Brad. *I can get almost 100% on 'Chemical Warfare' and that's a tough song, I'll open with that.* Brad said his goodbyes and hurried off, already preparing himself mentally.

"Hang on, who's Melvyn?" he heard Lauren saying as he was walking off.

*

When Brad got to the club-room, he felt a thrill of excitement. It was indeed Guitar Hero 6 that Kevin and Seth were playing. Evan was relaxing on a couch, watching disinterestedly and occasionally wincing at Kevin's enthusiastic but clumsy efforts.

"Hey Brad," said Kevin. "You wanna take over? Seth is crushing me here, I'll play again when Bernard gets back and I'm not the worst in the room." With a smile, Brad grabbed the controller and slung the strap over his shoulder. He quickly changed the difficulty up to Expert, and Seth looked at him askance.

"I'm more of a 'Medium' kinda guy," said Seth. "Evan, you wanna tag back in?"

"Might as well," said Evan, hopping to his feet. "Brad here looks like he knows what he's doing"

"Guest picks the song?" said Brad as he rushed through the menu down to Slayer's 'Chemical Warfare'.

"You mind picking something harder?" asked Evan. "It's a bit boring to do songs I can 100%"

"Don't be so douchey, Evan," said Kevin. "Brad, you pick whatever song you want and if it's too easy for Evan then I'll come jog his elbow."

Brad ignored the banter, selected his song of choice and set himself to get started. He quickly got into a rhythm; his score was close to perfect. To his irritation it still wasn't good enough; Kevin had delivered on his promise to jog Evan's elbow, but that was the only time Evan had missed a note.

"Nice work Brad," said Evan. "You ran me close. Best challenge I've ever had in this club-room."

"Thank you," said Brad, but something about Evan's graciousness touched a raw nerve. "But I know one thing you don't know," Brad continued.

"And what's that?" asked Evan, still grinning.

"I am not left-handed," said Brad, swinging the strap around to reverse the guitar. A look of shock flitted across Evan's features for a moment, but he spread his feet into a firmer stance, took a deep breath and braced himself. Brad still had the guest's right to choose songs, and went straight for 'Fury of the storm' by Dragonforce. Evan exhaled forcefully, intent on the screen. Brad just whistled nonchalantly and looked around the room.

The song began. Evan launched into frenetic activity as he strove to better his efforts. Brad, indeed left-handed, flailed ineffectually, barely hitting a single note. It was a full minute before Evan diverted his attention enough to realise that Brad had just been messing with him.

*

James Green: as president of WARP, I am proud to announce that after one day, our o-week recruitment scoreboard is as follows:
      1st place: Nathan with 15 total recruitments, 8 girls
      2nd place: Melvyn with 9 total recruitments, 3 girls
      3rd place: Tarryn with 4 total recruitments but she bribed like 10 people with lunch
17 January 2011
1 comment: **Evan Pretorius**: Wait, who's Melvyn?

Chapter 11

Jamie "Bradford" Rogers is now friends with **Melvyn Rahatni**
Melvyn Rahatni: Give a man a fish and he'll be like 'Ew. Fish.' Teach a man to fish and he'll be like 'Ugh. Fishing'.
18 January 2011

*

"Remind me why we're going in so early," said Kevin blearily, rubbing his eyes.

"It's our turn to help set up the stall," explained Brad. "So we need to get there first thing." Brad nodded toward a pair of travel mugs in his car's cupholders. "I brought coffee." Kevin grabbed one of the cups.

"Gonna need it," said Kevin, taking a sip. "I haven't woken up this early since the holidays started."

"It shows," said Brad. "I just hope you're excited for your first go at recruiting."

"I don't really know what to expect," said Kevin, shrugging. "I guess I just sit there and talk to people, how bad can it be?" Brad nodded.

"It's a little tougher than that," said Brad with a wry grin. "But don't worry, I'll show you how it's done."

*

"This guy looks geeky," said Kevin." Brad, talk to him,"

"You talk to him," said Brad. "I got the last one."

"Yeah but he didn't even respond. He just walked past."

"Still counts," said Brad.

"Well this one's gone past now," said Kevin. "Keep your eyes open for another target. Try this guy."

"No way," said Brad. "He's wearing a golf shirt. Much too preppy for WARP."

"It's a numbers game, Brad. The more people we talk to, the more we'll sign up."

"Kevin, you haven't talked to anyone in half an hour."

"That's not true," said Kevin. "We've only been here twenty-five minutes. And I almost signed up a girl earlier!"

"She was just asking for directions," said Brad. "And she walked off with your pen."

"That's fine," said Kevin, taking a sip of water. "I never liked that pen anyway. And those directions were wrong."

"Look, our shift's just about over," said Brad. "I think I see Seth on his way here. You reckon he'll do any better than us?"

"Well, he can hardly do any worse," said Kevin, examining his clipboard. "Looks like we signed up two people. Wait, no, those are our own forms. None. We signed up none."

"So how'd you guys do?" Seth asked as he approached the table.

"Two," said Kevin, standing up and clutching his clipboard to his chest. "We signed up two."

"Oh well," said Seth. "Better than striking out completely, I suppose. Either of you keen to stick around and help me out?" he continued as he manoeuvred himself behind the stall to take over Brad's seat.

"I think I've had enough embarrassment for the day, thank you," said Kevin. "So I'm off to the club-room. You coming, Brad?"

"I'll catch up," said Brad, pulling out his bathroom map. "Gotta make a pitstop first."

*

When Brad eventually got to the club-room, he got his first look at Tara, the girl Bernard had dated on-and-off for most of the last year. She was short, with dark skin and straight black hair. She was also snuggling up to Kevin on the couch, ignoring the venomous looks Bernard occasionally shot their way from the corner of the room. Kevin was clearly enjoying the attention, even if he seemed as surprised about it as anyone else.

On the other side of the room, Nathan was scowling as he fell further and further behind Evan in a game of Guitar Hero.

"So tell me Kevin," Tara said sweetly. "What did you do during your holiday?"

"Not too much," said Kevin, shrugging. "I started playing Magic the Gathering and did a bunch of reading."

"That sounds fun," said Tara. "You should teach me sometime."

"I'm not sure you could learn," Bernard interjected. "Reading isn't for everyone." Tara turned away from Kevin long enough to snarl at Bernard. Kevin attempted to break the tension by changing topic.

"What did everyone else do in their holidays?" he asked, looking around the room. Brad had dumped his bag and settled onto the couch opposite Kevin and Tara.

"Well, I went on a fishing trip to the Vaal with my dad," said Brad. "Caught some decent-sized trout."

"Huh, coincidence," said Evan. His points lead over Nathan was large enough that he could safely divert his attention from Guitar Hero. "I went ocean fishing with Tarryn down in Cape Town. Turns out Tarryn hates fishing so I went out by myself. Caught myself a barracuda. Turns out Tarryn hates eating fish, so I let him go."

"That's nothing," said Nathan, abandoning a lost cause and putting aside the guitar. "I ventured into the frigid Northern Ocean," he said with a faraway look in his eyes. "There, I caught the mighty Kraken. But I didn't return with it as a trophy. Instead I used it as bait for something larger still. It took patience and cunning but finally, after weeks of fierce struggle, I caught Bernard's mom."

*

James Green: After two days of recruiting, Nathan has a solid lead with 21 total recruitments, 10 of them girls. Special mention goes to Seth for getting two existing members to drop out.
19 January 2011

1 comment: **Seth Feynman**: They called R2-D2 a robot! We don't want their money.

"Don't try make any independent decisions," said Nathan. They were sitting at the stall awaiting the main stream of first years. "Just follow my lead."

It wasn't long before Brad got an opportunity to do exactly that. With neatly-trimmed curly hair and thin-framed glasses, a prospective member stood at the stall, looking at a manga he had picked up from the table.

"So what's this club all about?" came the inevitable question.

"We play tabletop games," said Nathan. "We also watch anime," he continued, glancing over at Brad, prompting him to keep going.

"We read comics," said Brad.

"We play console games," added Nathan.

"We play card games," said Brad.

"We dry-clean for the mafia," added Nathan.

"We host monthly LANs," added Brad. "But mostly we're a social group that hangs out and relaxes in our club-room."

"That sounds awesome," said the prospective member, albeit with a slightly puzzled look on his face. "But I don't think I'm gonna have much time for clubs this year."

"Don't worry about it," said Nathan reassuringly. "Not everyone can manage academics alongside a social life. If your syllabus looks tough then it's best that you focus on academics." Affronted, the prospective member drew himself up to his full height and reached for a pen.

"I'm not worried about that," he said. "I just have a lot of hobbies, you know? I mean, I got great Matric marks with no studying so I think I'll have plenty of free time."

"Well then," said Nathan, perking up. "If you're that smart you'll be just fine. And hey, if you sign up now and then realise you're too busy, you can always deregister later on."

Nathan maintained his sunny disposition until the guy had signed up. Moments later, however, he returned to his usual scornful demeanour.

"That is one moron we won't be seeing again," he said. "And good riddance."

*

"Are you guys sure about this?" Brad asked. "This stuff doesn't seem like it'll appeal to many people."

"That's fine," said James, waving away the question. "It's Thursday, Brad. We've already signed up everyone from the anime and comic book crowd. We might as well use the rest of the week to recruit the kind of guys who consider DnD too mainstream. Now give me a hand. This chainmail is heavier than I remembered."

As Brad helped James, Seth stood waiting nearby, swishing his foam sword and adjusting the Velcro straps on his much more practical aluminium body armour, which was styled like that of a Roman Legionary.

Bernard was smoking a cigarette, leaning on a heavily duct-taped two-handed great-sword, the grey foam flexing under his weight. Brad wasn't sure what Bernard was dressed as, with a big leather overcoat and battered tin helmet. They were out on the library lawn and Brad was feeling a bit self-conscious about all the glances that passersby threw toward the group.

James had his chainmail settled and was fiddling with his helmet's leather chinstrap when Nathan walked up to the group and raised an eyebrow at the ridiculous state of affairs.

"Hey James," said Nathan. "The Dark Ages called. They want their junk back." With that, Nathan shoved James just hard enough to send him toppling over backwards, windmilling his arms and yelping in distress.

This seemed a bit excessive to Brad, but Bernard and Seth laughed uproariously at the sight of James writhing around like an overturned turtle. Brad moved to help James up, but Nathan put out a hand to stop him.

"Give him a minute," said Nathan. "He might make it on his own."

"We should really help him up," said Brad. "He looks like he might strain something."

"I'm fine," said James from the floor.

"If he can't get up on his own then he's not allowed to use that armour at an actual LARP event," added Seth. "Safety rule."

"Don't worry guys, I got this," said James from the floor, digging in his heels to push himself toward a nearby tree.

"Any of you guys see Tron over the holidays?" asked Seth, after a brief pause.

"Yeah," said Nathan. "Was that supposed to be a movie, or just some sort of a test to see if Olivia Wilde is hot enough to sell tickets to a glorified light show?"

"Oh, she definitely is," said James, trying to reach behind his head to get a grip on the tree trunk. "I saw it three times."

"James," said Nathan. "You seriously need a girlfriend." James just sighed.

"I really do," he said contemplatively. "I wonder what I'm doing wrong?" he pondered aloud as he used the tree-trunk for leverage to try roll himself over.

"Hey Bernard," said Seth while they waited. "You up for a bout while James tries to get upright?"

"Might as well," said Bernard, stubbing his cigarette on his wooden buckler.

"Wait, you guys really fight?" said Brad. "I thought this was sort of a DnD thing but with costumes."

"A man needs more excitement than just rolling dice, Brad," said James, now flipped over onto his stomach and trying to press himself up, without success. "This is Live Action Role Play. We get to actually beat on each other."

"Sounds dangerous," said Brad. Bernard shook his head.

"No, dude, this stuff is Latex and styrofoam. I couldn't hurt someone with this if they let me."

"Maybe yours, Bernard," declared James, who had managed to get up to a kneeling position and was leaning against the tree trunk and taking a breather before the final push. "Mine is a plus four adamant great sword forged by the master smith, Hayes the Dwarf. This thing would kill you in two hits." Brad covered his face with his hand.

Finally on his feet, James noticed Brad's expression and raised his hands defensively.

"Hey, I'm not crazy, just in character. Now who wants a bout?"

Seth and Bernard were waving their weapons toward each other ineffectually, neither willing to get close enough to get hit.

"Stop messing around," said James, striding toward them. "I'll show you how it's done." With that, he raised his foam sword high overhead and took a heavy swing at Bernard, who lifted his own weapon to deflect the hit. He was only partially successful; the impact knocked his sword from his grip, and James moved in for a follow-up blow. Bernard, however, had the enormous advantage of no longer being armed and a gentle one-handed shove was enough to send James sprawling.

"He's further from the tree this time," commented Nathan.

*

Chapter 12

Suresh "Kevinford" Singh is in a relationship with **Tara Gounder**:
24 January 2011
1 comment: **James Green**: No key for you!

*

"Good lord," said Kevin, staring out the passenger window as Brad negotiated the Empire road traffic on the way to West. "Look at the queue on the M1 South over there." Brad glanced in the direction Kevin had indicated and shook his head ruefully. Johannesburg was in the middle of a summer storm and the wet weather was having a disastrous effect on traffic. The M1 highway crossed over Empire road up ahead, and it was packed solid with no sign of movement.

"I'd hate to be stuck in that," said Brad. "We'll be late to Evan's campaign as it is." It was Monday morning and the first day of term, but more importantly it was their first roleplaying session of the year. Evan's campaign was in the traditional Dungeons and Dragons medieval setting, and Brad would be playing as a Lawful Good Paladin named Brendon the Stoic. Finally getting through the last of the traffic, Brad's patience wore thin as he searched for parking.

By the time he and Kevin got to the club-room they were cold and damp despite their umbrellas and it was ten minutes after the game's start time. Matt had arrived only moments before them and was unpacking for the session. Seth was in the process of putting together his elaborate arrangement of dice and snacks. Bernard's character sheet and dice were already lying on the table while the man himself was sleeping with his feet propped up next to them. On the couches were a small group of first years sitting with Lauren, all intent on their phones. Brad's eyes skipped over them and he took his seat at the table.

"Evan isn't here yet," said Seth. "He texted me, he says he's stuck in traffic on the M1. But you are just in time to witness the unveiling of the new and improved Mordak McGee," he continued, pulling a sheet of paper out of his bag and holding it aloft.

"I've been writing backstory and trawling optimization forums since we stopped this campaign for the holidays. This character sheet is a masterpiece."

Brad looked quizzically at the sheet of paper in Seth's hands. It didn't look much like a Dnd character sheet. Seth noticed too. The blood drained from his face as he realised what he was holding.

"These are my personal details for registration," Seth said in a hoarse voice. "I must have handed in the wrong character sheet at faculty office." As Seth put his head in his hands, the door swung open and James walked in.

"So it's a new year," he announced. "Who failed what, and how bad?"

"Seth messed up his registration," Brad started to explain, but James stopped him.

"Don't change the subject Brad. I know you failed Customary Law. I passed it, for those of you who are interested." He clapped Brad on the shoulder paternally. "Brad, if you need any help the second time around, I can take a break from my second year classes to give you a few pointers."

"Sure thing," said Brad. "If I need advice on how to switch degrees every year 'til I'm twenty one I know who to ask. Meanwhile, Seth has an issue here."

"I took a gap year!" protested James. "And what's up with Seth?"

"I handed in my character sheet instead of my personal details for registration," explained Seth. James's eyes widened. Brad, meanwhile, was using the internet on his phone to do a bit of research.

"It's okay," said Brad. "The deadline for amending registration is still three days away." James and Seth ignored him.

"This is a disaster," said James. "What's your plan?"

"It's not a big deal," Brad tried to explain again. "He can just submit an amendment of registration form at the faculty office."

"I don't even have a plan yet," said Seth. "I'm still shocked I did something so stupid."

"Well Evan isn't gonna be here for ages," said James. "Let's head over to Faculty office and see what we can do. Matt, you hold down the fort. The rest of us are heading out. Don't let the blonde shed on the couch too much."

"You should write up a girlfriend sheet," muttered Lauren.

*

"Well, I really can't give you back your registration documents." This heartbreaking news was delivered by a very helpful lady administrator at the reception desk, in the engineering faculty office. "But there's no need to worry," she said with a smile, sliding a form across the table. "You can just fill in this amendment of registration form and we can sort it all out." Seth stared blankly at the form for a few moments until Kevin nudged him in the side, prompting him to take the form with a brittle smile and turn to leave. In silence, Brad, James and Kevin followed him out.

With a sigh, Seth sat down heavily on the steps outside the engineering faculty, not noticing the light rain gradually soaking his clothes and his amendment of registration form.

"I've been playing that character for three years," Seth said slowly, staring down at his feet. "I've spent more time on it than on my degree."

"No sense sitting here and getting wet," said Kevin, holding out a hand to help Seth up. "We might as well head back to the club-room. We'll put on the heater and figure this out."

*

It began to sink in for Brad what it meant to really be a geek. To anyone but him, Seth's character sheet was worthless. Dnd would never make Seth rich, or popular. He'd never get a girl or impress people by designing a perfect character. Being a geek meant caring about things out of pure intellectual interest regardless of real-world value.

Brad wouldn't be affected the same way if he lost Brendon the Stoic, but he felt Seth's pain and wanted to help.

They were back in the club-room, brainstorming ways to get the character sheet back. So far, all they'd concluded was that stealing it was not an option.

"I still think stealing it is an option," said Bernard.

"No it isn't," said James. "My permanent record has a few too many black marks already. I'm not willing to risk another Disciplinary hearing just because Seth screwed up."

"I'll help," said Brad. "My permanent record is clean, the risk isn't so bad for me."

"Yeah, me too," said Kevin.

"I've got nothing better to do," said Bernard, shrugging.

"Fine, you guys steal the sheet," said James, sighing. "But I'm just the lookout."

"Thanks guys," said Seth. "This means a lot to me."

"Yes, yes," said James. "Emotions are wonderful. Let's get on with the planning, I don't have all day."

*

Brad and Seth tried to look nonchalant as they walked into the faculty office and got into the short queue at the reception desk. Fire alarm sirens rang out, turning the faculty office into a seething mass of activity. Brad and Seth rushed to the reception desk.

"Quick!" said Seth to the same administrator he'd spoken to earlier. "Pass us the documents you need to save; we'll help you carry everything out!"

"Not necessary, thank you" she replied calmly. "I sent everything to Senate House this morning. Now please exit in an orderly manner through the doors behind you, and evacuate the building using the fire exit to your right. Seth shot Brad a pained look and they filed out with everyone else.

*

Kevin and James were waiting for them outside the building; Bernard was lying on the ground being treated for possible smoke inhalation by a pretty female paramedic.

"No luck?" asked Kevin, seeing Brad and Seth emerge empty-handed. Seth just shook his head.

"The documents have already been sent to Senate House for data capture," explained Brad.

"Yeah," said Seth. "There's not much chance of stealing anything from the data centre. It's access-controlled and there are security guards all over the building."

"Let's see if Bernard's okay," suggested James. "And figure out how to get into the data centre in Senate House."

"Bernard might really need that oxygen mask," said Kevin. "You should have seen him running after he pulled that fire alarm. It was like the rolling boulder scene in Raiders." They walked over to where Bernard was lying, oxygen mask over his face. The paramedic had moved off to attend to a guy who had twisted his ankle running out of the building.

"Hey guys," said Bernard, pulling the mask off. "You guys get the sheet?" he asked, still breathing heavily.

"Afraid not," said Brad. "Seth looks like he has a plan, though." As he listened, Bernard put the oxygen mask back on.

"We've got one option left," said Seth. "If we apply for data capture jobs in Senate House, we'll get access to those registration sheets. And hey, we can make a little money in the deal."

"Would West really hire random students just like that?" asked Brad.

"West will hire anyone," said James. "You'd have realised that by now if you went to some classes. Any one of us can get a job like that."

"He's right," said Seth. "In First Year our Health and Safety lecturer was actually a caterer who'd gotten lost on campus. We should all apply though," he continued. "Just to make sure. West has low standards, but they do lose a lot of paperwork."

"You guys go on ahead," said Bernard. "I'm gonna rest up here and then head home, I'm parked pretty close. I'll send in my CV tonight."

*

Leaving Bernard behind, they walked back to WARP. The rain had stopped and the sun was up, making for a surreal scene as the bright sun reflected off of the myriad deep puddles. As they approached the club-room door, Brad heard Evan's voice coming from inside the room.

"Hey Evan," said Brad.

"Hey guys. Sorry I couldn't make it to the session; a truck jack-knifed on the M1. They had to close off the whole highway and I was stuck for three hours. If you guys are all free, I can skip my afternoon tut and we can do the session now."

"Nah," said Brad. "Bernard's still down at the ambulance and we couldn't get Seth's character sheet back from faculty anyway."

"Oh ok," said Evan. He then blinked in confusion. "Wait, what? I can't make sense of any of that."

Together, Brad, Seth, Kevin and James filled Evan in on the morning's events. Evan's eyes lit up as he heard the story, but then after a thoughtful silence his shoulders slumped.

"Guys, I'm sorry to say this and I'm as disappointed as you are, but we don't need an elaborate plan. There's a simple solution."

*

"I actually did the exact same thing when I was an undergrad," Professor Ndlovu explained as she handed Seth his coffee-stained character sheet. "You would not believe some of the stunts I pulled to get mine back," she said, shaking her head ruefully. "I wish I'd thought of just asking a lecturer who plays DnD."

Chapter 13

Evan Pretorius is now single
3 February 2011
2 comments: **Evan Pretorius**: and women across the land rejoiced
Nathan Hillary: Tarryn's mom is happy, that's for sure

*

"Seatbelt," said Brad, prompting Kevin to squirm around to buckle up while without putting down his phone. "You texting Tara?" Brad asked once Kevin had his seatbelt on.

"Nah," said Kevin, holding up his phone's screen to show Brad his Facebook home page. "Did you know Evan broke up with Tarryn?" he asked. Brad sat bolt upright at this news.

"Oh yeah?" asked Brad. "Any idea why?"

"Not a clue," said Kevin. "I guess you'll have to ask him. I do know that Tara's already trying to set Tarryn up with some guy friend of hers." Brad's jaw tightened.

"It's a bit soon for that, isn't it?" he commented. Kevin shrugged.

"If you're volunteering to tell her that, go ahead," he said. "I know not to argue with Tara." Kevin went back to tapping away at his phone. "Listen, Brad," he said. "I know you're not normally big on parties and drinking but I figure we should take Evan out for a few drinks tonight at McGinty's. You know, for a guy's night after his breakup."

"Yeah, sure thing," said Brad, distracted.

"Uh, Brad?" asked Kevin.

"Yeah?"

"You can drive now."

*

Brad day-dreamed through his Customary Law lecture that morning, thinking through what he'd say to Tarryn in the club-room later. *I should be sympathetic, but play it cool. The key is letting her know I'm interested without putting any pressure on her.*

"Scientific curiosity is of crucial importance to tertiary education in any field," Dr. Johnson was saying, but Brad was obliviously staring out a window.

I've got to be a good friend first and foremost, thought Brad. *I'll wait for her to make the first move.* "And that is why," Dr. Johnson continued, walking around and collecting test scripts. "I'm timing how long it takes this blonde guy to notice we're writing a test," she finished, watching Brad curiously, stopwatch app running on her phone.

Breaking out of his reverie, Brad nodded decisively to himself. It was too soon to push the issue, but he'd use the opportunity to get close to Tarryn. Brad checked his watch to see how much time was left before he could head to WARP.

Fifteen minutes is far too long, thought Brad, and he began to fidget until he saw a sheet of paper in front of him. Looking up, he noticed the whole class was writing, except for a few who had finished and were watching him intently.

Fifteen minutes isn't nearly long enough, thought Brad, starting to write furiously.

*

I might actually have passed that, thought Brad as he walked out of the lecture venue. His heart was still pounding from the shock of seeing that test in front of him and it wasn't slowing down as he made his way to the club-room. When he got there he looked quickly around the room, only to be disappointed. Tarryn was normally there during lunch-break, but not this time. Brad shrugged off his disappointment; she'd probably be around later on and there was plenty to keep him busy in the club-room.

The room was crowded with first years, as often happened early in the year. Older WARPlings perched in various corners of the room, staring at the first-years with varying degrees of distaste. On his way through the room he stopped next to the table, where Seth was trying ineptly to teach Magic the Gathering to Claudia, the girl Nathan had argued with at O-Week.

"No Claudia, that ability stays on the stack even if its source is removed from play," he said for the third time.

"What the fuck is the stack?" she asked for the third time.

"Hey Seth," said Brad. All the seats in the room were taken, so he stood awkwardly next to Seth's chair.

"Hey Brad," said Seth. "This is Claudia. She's learning to play Magic."

"Well I would be," said Claudia. "If you would stop countering my spells long enough to explain what the stack is."

"I'm pretty sure I explained," said Seth. "Spells and abilities are placed on the stack when cast, activated or triggered and each player must pass priority before an effect on the stack will resolve." Claudia stared blankly at Seth. So did Brad, for that matter, despite having played enough casual Magic to know most of the basics.

"Hi Claudia," said Brad. "It's nice to see you found your way to the club-room."

"No thanks to you guys," said Claudia. "I had to try calling Nathan to ask him how to get here, and it turns out he gave me someone else's number. Ari was very helpful though." Brad tried to hold back a grin. Nathan didn't like people hassling him so he gave out Ari's phone number instead of his own except with people he had a good reason to talk to.

"Speaking of Nathan," said Brad. "Should we invite him out to McGinty's tonight?"

"Yeah, might as well" said Seth. "You wanna send him a text?" Brad pulled out his phone and did just that as he made his way across the rest of the room to where Kevin was sitting, eyeing the first-years nervously.

"I can't believe I was ever that young," said Kevin, shaking his head ruefully.

"Kevin, you started university a year early," said Brad. "You still are that young."

"It's the experiences that matter," said Kevin, laughing.

"Speaking of which," said Brad. "Any idea how Tarryn is taking the breakup?"

"Not a clue," said Kevin, shrugging. "She hasn't been around. Stop worrying about Tarryn, she has other friends. We're only responsible for Evan. Worry about your liver instead, it's gonna take a beating tonight."

*

"Two beers!" said Evan as he ordered the second round of the evening.

"Actually I'll have a coffee," Brad said to the barman. "I'm driving."

"You heard the man," said Evan. "Two beers and a coffee."

Mcginty's was a quiet pub and bar in the Northern suburbs of Joburg, catering to nominally cash-strapped students from upmarket neighbourhoods. It was quiet, which suited the WARP group, and not too expensive, which suited their pockets.

Brad walked back to the dark wood table where Kevin and Seth were still nursing their beers from earlier and sat down. With a beer in each hand and a look of intense concentration, Evan used his elbows to pull out a chair while Bernard attacked a plate of chicken wings.

"Does Bernard know that those things have bones?" Brad asked, but Bernard didn't slow down at all.

"Does Bernard know that he's on fire?" asked Evan. This time Bernard did react, freezing for a moment before frantically patting himself down, starting with his beard.

"He never stops falling for that one," said Seth, laughing. Bernard fixed him with a stern look.

"One time it was true," said Bernard. "A man doesn't forget a thing like that."

"I suppose not," said Kevin, downing the last of his beer. "Is anyone else coming?"

"I texted Nathan this afternoon," said Brad. "Let me see if I got a reply." Brad pulled out his phone and checked his messages; there was indeed a reply, saying 'Tutoring until late, be there around 6.'

"It's six fifteen now," said Seth, looking at his watch. Before he could say anything more, the door swung open.

"Thanks for the invite, Brad," said Ari as he walked in. "Nice place," he said, looking around. "I like the wood panelling; makes for a nice old-timey feel. It's too bad you and Tarryn didn't work out," he continued, patting Evan on the shoulder. "But you know what they say: there are hotter fish in the sea."

"Uh...thanks?" said Evan.

"No problem," said Ari. "Now let's get you a drink." Evan gestured with his two beers and raised his eyebrows.

"No, I mean a real drink," said Ari. "Come on."

*

Brad woke up the next day with a splitting headache. He winced at the bright sunlight streaming through his curtains, and sat up with a groan. His groan was echoed by another groan from the floor next to his bed. Swinging his legs over the side, Brad used both hands to push himself to his feet to look for the source of the sound.

"What happened?" said Evan, blinking up at him blearily from the sleeping bag he was tangled in. "Look for clues. Where are we?"

"This is my house," said Brad. "I don't remember getting here though." He stood up and walked to his dressing table. "Keys, cellphone, wallet. Mine are all here. Have you got yours?" Evan rummaged in a pile of belongings on the desk next to where he had been sleeping.

"I think I have extras," he said. "I don't recognise half this stuff," he continued, holding up a keychain with a pair of fist-sized fluffy dice. "Who even makes fluffy D20s?"

"What I don't understand," said Brad. "Is what happened to me. I ordered nothing but coffee all night, how'd I get into this state?" Evan grabbed a handful of till slips and started peering at them one at a time.

"These all say 'Irish Coffee', so that answers that." Moments later, Jarryd stuck his head in the door.

"Hey fatty, I...what?" for once he was momentarily speechless. "I know mom and dad went to fetch you late last night, but I had no idea they were bringing home strays."

"This must be the family pet," said Evan, grinning. "He has such healthy teeth. What brand of kibble do you use?"

"And why aren't you at school, anyway?" added Brad.

"Mom said I could take the day off to make fun of you," Jarryd replied, but Brad didn't take the bait and just stared him down. "Got a doctor's note," said Jarryd, waving a slip of paper. "Says I have the 'flu."

*

"Your brother's right about one thing," said Evan, flapping the midriff of an oversize t-shirt. Brad was driving them to West and Evan was in the passenger seat, looking a bit uncomfortable in the ill-fitting clothes he'd had to borrow from Brad. "You really should join the gym. Annual fee is pretty cheap and it's got all the basic equipment you'll need." Brad eyed him sideways through the dark glasses he was wearing, and reached for his travel mug.

"I'll think about it," he said. "But not today. The one thing I haven't figured out is what my parents were using the spare bedroom for. I'd have thought they'd put you in there rather than giving you a sleeping bag."

"That is odd," said Evan. "I'm still trying to figure out whose stuff that was on your desk. Anyway, I have to head off to class. See you around, Brad."

It was the middle of the third lecture slot of the day and WARP was mostly empty when Brad got there, with only Nathan and Seth in the room.

"I hear last night was quite something," said Nathan. "It's pretty low of you, making a move so soon after their breakup." Brad spun around to face Nathan.

"Wait, Tarryn was there?" he said, eyes wide.

"Who said anything about Tarryn?" said Nathan, laughing.

*

Mary "Jamie's mom" Rogers: Jamie, dear, I hope you and your friends got to university okay this morning.
>4 February 2011
>>1 comment: **Aristos Hadjigeorgio**: Two out of three isn't bad. Nice house by the way, but how do I get out?

Chapter 14

Nathan Hillary: Baby skin isn't as soft as people say. Either that, or this rug is a fake.

        14 February 2011

*

"What are your plans for Valentine's day?" Brad asked. "Anything interesting?" It was a sunny morning and Brad was inching his way through traffic. Construction on Empire Road severely congested their route, giving them plenty of time to fill with conversation.

"I'm a little broke right now," replied Kevin. "I've got most of the cards I want for my Affinity deck, but it's been an expensive process." Brad shook his head ruefully.

"I can't believe the price of some of those cards," he said. "Magic is an expensive hobby."

"It's not that bad," said Kevin. "All my decks together cost half as much as your brother's bicycle."

"That's different," said Brad. "A bicycle is more than just printed cardboard."

"The value of a thing is in what it lets you do," said Kevin. "Money's just printed paper when you get down to it. Your brother's bike lets him race, my decks make me competitive in tournaments."

"I suppose it makes sense," said Brad, shrugging. "Let's just see what Tara thinks of getting a hand-made valentine's gift right after you spent a thousand rand on 4 cards." Kevin grimaced.

"Don't remind me," said Kevin. "How about you? You got anyone in mind as a valentine?"

"Not really," said Brad, flushing.

"I see how it is," said Kevin. "Too embarrassed to admit you have a crush on Tarryn, huh?"

"What?" Brad protested. "It's not like that!"

"Sure it isn't," said Kevin with a wry grin. "That's why you're turning the same colour you do when the elevator's broken and we have to use the stairs."

*

The club-room's blinds were drawn against the bright sun, leaving the room dim and gloomy. As his eyes adapted to the light, Brad glanced quickly around but saw no sign of Tarryn. She hadn't been in the club-room since the breakup. Brad had begun thinking about calling her. He'd hoped to run into her casually; a phone call would feel pressured.

Bernard was asleep on the couch with his face covered by an old pizza box. Seth was at the table, intent on his laptop while James and Melvyn were playing a game of chess next to him. Kevin walked in behind Brad.

"Hey guys," said Brad as he sat down on a couch opposite Bernard. "I got Evan's message; did he tell any of you why he cancelled the game today?"

"He's spending Valentine's day with some girl instead," said Seth, shaking his head ruefully. "And for the rest of us? No dates AND no DnD. I always thought it was one or the other."

"It hasn't even been two weeks since he broke up with Tarryn," said Brad. "Isn't it a bit soon?"

"Don't be such a prude," said James. "Not everyone here is a teenage choir boy."

"It was a brass band," Brad protested. "And I'm almost twenty!"

"Two weeks is a bit too quick," said Kevin. "Feelings are still a bit sensitive."

"Quiet, Kevin," said James. "You're even younger, what do you know?"

"Tell us more about this brass band," said Melvyn.

"I might not be a relationship expert," Kevin said. "But I'm the only guy here who has a girlfriend."

"Tara doesn't count," said James, with Seth nodding in agreement. "She dated Bernard. That makes her the only person alive with standards as low as this university." Seth nodded more vigorously, and Bernard followed his lead.

"Hey!" said Bernard with a frown, after a few moments thinking. "Getting with Tara was way tougher. West doesn't get mad when I don't show up for a couple of months."

"Let's get back to that thing about a brass band," suggested Melvyn.

"The point being," said James. "Two weeks is long enough to start showing interest in someone else, especially with Valentine's day involved. Which is why we need to know if you've made it out of the friendzone with Tarryn."

"Why do you all think I'm interested in Tarryn?" Brad demanded, blushing bright red. "There's nothing between us, she's just a friend!"

"Booyah!" said James, high-fiving Seth. "Safest bet we ever made, Seth."

"Yeah," said Seth. "A little too safe. Most of the club bet the same way."

"So how much did we each win?" Kevin asked. Brad shot him a look of betrayal and Kevin shrugged sheepishly. Seth pulled up a spreadsheet on his laptop.

"Well," said Seth. "There were ten bets against Brad, and only one for him."

"What can I say?" said Melvyn, shrugging. "I had faith in my boy Bradford. Have fun dividing up my fifty bucks. Now can we talk about this brass band?"

*

"It's intrusive, is all I'm saying," said Brad. "I mean, I don't see anyone interfering in things between you and Tara." Brad was driving out of West early. His afternoon lecture had been cancelled because the lecturer hadn't been sure what subject he was supposed to teach. Kevin was skipping his last lecture to try come up with something for Tara before that evening.

"I don't know about that," said Kevin. "James put me on a suicide watchlist as soon as he found out we were dating."

"That's just sensible," said Brad. "Look at Bernard, he's an absolute mess." Kevin shrugged.

"It's hardly fair to attribute that to Tara," said Brad. "According to Seth, Bernard's parents are genetically identical."

"The point is," said Brad, trying to get back on topic. "I don't have a crush on Tarryn, and if I did, it has absolutely nothing to do with the rest of WARP. Not that it matters anyway, since I don't."

"Yeah Brad, that sounds believable," said Kevin, laughing. Brad frowned.

"Just drop it, okay?"

"Well, if you say you don't have a crush on her," said Kevin. "I guess I'll take you at your word."

"That's all I'm asking for," said Brad. "And listen, if you want to borrow some cash to get Tara something, it's not a problem."

"I wouldn't dream of it," protested Kevin. "It just wouldn't feel right."

"It's really nothing," said Brad. "I know you're good for it."

"You don't know that," said Kevin. "I don't even know that. Look, it's fine, I'll figure something out, okay."

"As long as you're sure," said Brad. "From what I've heard, she has a reputation for drama when she isn't getting the attention she wants." Kevin just shrugged ruefully.

*

"No date, huh?" Jarryd asked, as Brad dropped his bag next to the kitchen table and headed for the fridge.

"And what of it?" asked Brad as he stoically avoided looking at the box of doughnuts on the bottom shelf. "You're here too."

"Jamie, West University has over ten thousand women. I go to an all-boys school." With a twinge of regret, Brad reached for a lunchbox full of chicken salad and went to sit next to his brother.

"Nice choice," said Jarryd approvingly. "You wouldn't want those doughnuts anyway, I licked them earlier."

"Of course you did," said Brad with a wry grin. "You know that once rowing season's over, you'll have to dial back on your eating too." Jarryd shrugged.

"Yeah I guess so. Rugby won't be quite the same workload," said Jarryd.

"You're dateless now, while you're in shape," said Brad. "Just imagine if you get fat." Jarryd winced.

"At least with rowing out of the way I'll have enough free time to actually meet some girls. Hey, if you're never actually gonna ask this Tarryn out, you should introduce me." Brad put his face in his hands and sighed.

"What is it with all you people? Why do you all think I have a crush on Tarryn?"

"It's how nerds work," replied Jarryd. "You sort of latch onto the nearest girl and hover around in hopes they make a move on you."

"And where does this alleged wisdom come from?" asked Brad. "You don't know any girls. Hell, you don't even know any nerds!"

"Hey man," said Jarryd defensively. "I watch TV. I see how things work. Plus I talked to Dad about it. He reckons you should just ask her out, get rejected, and get on with your life."

"Can you people stop trying to run my life?" said Brad, pushing away from the table. "Where is Dad anyway? If he wants to give me advice, he can say so to my face!"

"He's in his study, marking tests."

Angrily, Brad made his way up the stairs toward his father's study. Without knocking, he pushed open the door.

"So I hear you and Jarryd have been talking about me," said Brad. "I'm not sure how I feel about that."

Brad's father was sitting at a mahogany desk piled high with test papers.

"Sure, come on in," he said with a laugh, surreptitiously minimizing the Facebook tab he had open on his laptop. "Knocking is overrated anyway. Bad for the door. Take a seat, lad," said Elliot. "Now what's this that you're mad about?" As Brad pulled up a chair he found his anger deserting him. He had always found it difficult to stay angry at his father.

"Well, I wouldn't say that I'm mad about it," said Brad. "I'm just getting a bit fed up with how everyone keeps talking about my love life behind my back. Everyone at WARP is doing it, now you and Jarryd are at it as well."

"I can't speak for WARP," said Elliot. "Because I'm not sure what it is. But I can say that Jarryd came to have a chat with me because he was worried about you. He reckons you're getting hung up on a girl who isn't right for you, and that's not a good situation to be in."

"Why not talk to me about it directly?" asked Brad.

"That's what Jarryd suggested I do. But you're right that it really isn't our business, so I figured that if you wanted to talk about it then you'd come to me."

"So why gossip behind my back?"

"Jamie, I'm fifty six years old and I've been happily married for half of those," said Elliot. I have virtually no drama in my own life. It's either this or I start watching soapies." Jamie laughed out loud at the absurd mental image of his father watching a soap opera. "Speaking of happily married," Elliot continued. "I didn't get that way by accident. I happen to know a thing or two about the females of our species. A little advice never hurt anyone, so why don't you let me know what's going on, since you're here anyway?"

"Sounds like you already know most of it," said Brad.

"Ari filled me in on most of it that time you locked him in the house," said Elliot. "But I might as well get the full story from you."

"Well, it's like this," said Brad. "There's this girl, Tarryn. I suppose you could say I have a pretty bad crush on her, and I'm not really sure what to do about it."

"Well, first things first," said Elliot. "Do you really like this girl, or did you just imprint on her, like a lizard?"

"Of course I..." said Brad, pausing when his brain finally caught up to his mouth. "Wait, what was that about a lizard?"

"I've taught a lot of teenage boys over the years," explained Elliot. "So I know how their brains work, insofar as they do." Brad's brow crinkled, but he didn't interrupt. "It comes from watching too much TV. They feel like they're supposed to have a love interest for narrative purposes, so they latch onto the first girl they meet. As often as not, they don't even really like her, but they get fixated anyway."

"I do watch a lot of TV," admitted Brad. "I'll give it some thought," he continued. "What you say makes sense."

As Brad left he paused for a moment, just outside the door. From inside he heard his dad clicking his mouse, pulling up the Facebook page he'd hidden when Brad had walked in.

"Tarryn Park, huh? Jarryd was right, she's not even that hot," Elliot was muttering to himself. With a wry smile, Brad turned away and walked to his bedroom.

*

Jarryd Rogers: I can't believe I only won five bucks on that bet
14 February 2011

Chapter 15

Evan Pretorius: When Plan A fails, you try Plan B, but only as a distraction while you try Plan A again. Because Plan A is solid, man. That's why it's Plan A.
3 March 2011

*

Kevin lowered his phone to his lap. Then he turned it slowly around two or three times. Finally he put it in his pocket and stared blankly at the wall.

Kevin had always been highly introspective, but this looked bad. Whatever this news was, Kevin was not handling it well. Brad was debating whether to reach out to his friend or leave him be, when he noticed that Kevin's hands were trembling slightly. Before Brad could decide just how to phrase his question, Seth pre-empted him.

"Geez, Kevin, who died?" said Seth. Kevin seemed not to hear him, despair clearly visible on his face.

"It can't be that bad, whatever it is," said Bernard. "Tell us what's going on, we'll try to care."

Kevin just raised his hand and extended it toward Bernard. He looked at it for a while and then realised his phone was not in it. Finding it in his other hand, he passed it to Bernard.

Bernard read the message. For a few moments he just stared.

"Holy. Fucking. Shit," he said after a pause. He handed the phone to Seth, directing a meaningful glance at the group of first-years sitting on the couches chatting. He and Seth stood up and between them guided Kevin out into the corridor to talk privately. Brad followed them out.

"Don't panic, Kevin. You know how she is, it could be anybody's kid." said Evan. Bernard grunted in shock as he realised the implications of that statement."Holy. Fucking. Shit," he repeated.

"Bernard, you're in the clear," said Seth. "If it were yours, she'd be 4 months along, we'd have known sooner."

Kevin finally looked up from his catatonic state, grimacing in distaste.

"It isn't someone else's kid, okay?" he said quietly. "I'm sure of it."

*

Kevin's light-hearted life-style was under threat. Magic the Gathering strained Kevin's limited budget as it was. Child support would clean him out.

The group sat in grim silence.

"Look on the bright side," said Bernard. He stopped there. He had nothing. Seth had something on his mind, though.

"Think about this for a second, Kevin. What do we actually know?" he asked.

"That Tara is pregnant."

"No," said Seth. "What we do actually know which makes us believe that?"

"She took a pregnancy test, and it was fucking positive!" snapped Kevin.

Seth shook his head slowly and just pointed at Kevin's phone. Kevin sat up straight as he realised what Seth was getting at. "Oh, ok. You're right, we just have her messages." Seth nodded his approval. Brad was appalled at the implication:

"So what you're saying is she just said this to get attention? You think she's lying about being pregnant? Who does that?" he demanded incredulously.

"We already know she lies for attention," Evan pointed out. "Remember when she told us that her dad had thrown her out of the house, and she started sleeping in the club-room?" For the first time in his long tenure, Bernard felt an urge to clean WARP. But Evan wasn't done yet. "But her parents came looking for her the next day? Remember she told us all she's a lesbian? And how many guys has she dated? A pregnancy scare is just her sort of emo drama." Kevin drew himself up angrily, about to defend his girlfriend. After a moment, he exhaled heavily and slumped down.

"You might be right," he conceded. "But I can't just tell her I think she's lying. What if it's true? What if I end up telling the mother of my child that I don't trust her?"

"Agreed," said Seth. "It's a huge risk to take with no information. We need to verify her claim. Without her knowing we're doing it."

"We can't exactly trick her into taking a pregnancy test," replied Kevin. Before the words were out of his mouth, Evan leapt to his feet.

"Guys, chill. This is easy. All we need is urine."

*

Walking past Nino's often enough to keep an eye on Tara was teaching Brad one thing. Looking nonchalant is hard work. He'd been chosen for the surveillance role because Tara barely knew him, so the chances of him being recognised were minimal. It could have been worse, Bernard was on retrieval duty.

Brad walked nonchalantly past, nonchalantly, for the third time in half an hour and peeked into the coffee shop to see what the pair were up to. Kevin had positioned Tara with her back to the entrance to guarantee that she wouldn't spot their surveillance efforts, and he was plying her with hot chocolate and scones, making polite conversation and skirting the serious issues they'd met to discuss.

On Brad's fourth pass, he noted that Tara had drained her cup and was starting to get up, presumably to make her way to the bathroom. Brad had Evan's number already typed in, he just had to hit the call button.

*

Tara made her way up the stairs to the second floor of the matrix, where the bathrooms were located. She was aggrieved to note a 'closed for repairs' sign hanging on the door to the bathroom, but before she turned around to go find another, a pale, black-haired janitor, who reminded her of Seth, emerged and removed the sign. She glanced once more in his direction as he walked off. Seth could never grow such a luxuriant moustache.

Walking into the bathroom, she found that all but one of the stalls had 'out of order' signs. It was clear that some construction work had been going on, with building dust and other evidence of recent drilling scattered through the stall.

Not bothered, she did what she had to do. She noted that this upgraded toilet had the strangest flush mechanism she'd ever seen. No water went into the bowl when she pulled the lever. Instead, the contents of the bowl were just drained rapidly. It was as if a release valve had been opened on a pipe leading straight down. This must be what Bernard meant when he talked about all the water-saving toilets on campus.

*

Brad rushed to the alley behind the matrix.

"Retrieval was successful," Bernard informed him. "The sample is secure," he added, holding up a Tupperware container filled with clear yellow fluid. "Most of the sample," he amended with a grimace, wiping his sleeve with a Kleenex. Seth arrived on Brad's heels, peeling off his fake moustache.

"I've got the kit," said Seth, producing a home pregnancy test kit from a pocket of his overalls. "Let's get this going," he continued, dipping the white stick into the sample.

"Now we wait. Ten minutes, it says," explained Seth. An awkward silence ensued.

"So, Seth, how's engineering going?" asked Brad in an attempt to while away the minutes with small talk.

"Meh," responded Seth, shrugging.

"So Bernard, how about that pee, huh?"

"Meh," said Bernard, shrugging.

It was a long ten minutes. Once the results were in they spent another ten minutes arguing over who got to give Kevin the good news.

"It was my design, I should get to do it," was Seth's argument. "And besides, I had to buy the test kit and build the release valve."

"I got sample on me." Bernard had only the one argument, but it was a strong one, and he wasn't backing down an inch. Brad, realising that this could take all day, texted Kevin, and then went back inside to watch what happened.

"You know, Tara," said Kevin congenially, after looking at his phone. "I don't believe that you are pregnant." He then looked her in the eyes challengingly, a slight smile on his lips. Tara was dumbstruck.

"I took a test two days ago, and it came up positive!" she protested loudly, drawing looks from everyone in the coffee shop. Kevin leaned back and smiled.

"You took a test ten minutes ago," he said quietly. "And it came up negative."

*

Having locked up the club-room for the day, the group retired to Seth's house to celebrate. Seth produced a bottle of champagne and some glasses. It was cheap and it was flat, but it tasted of victory.

"So, Seth," Brad said after they had toasted one another's awesomeness and ingenuity. "Where'd Evan get to? Last I saw he was with you in the ladies' room, taking the release valve back out." A look of horror swept across Seth's face.

"Oh crud," said Seth, pulling at his collar in embarrassment. "The plan was that he'd hide in the stall until I could head back and put up a 'closed' sign so he could escape cleanly."

"So let's get back there and put it up," said Bernard, making shooing motions. Seth shook his head.

"We're all over the limit. We'll have to sober up before we drive back."

*

Chapter 16

Tarryn Park: 'Slut' is how we vilify a woman for exercising her right to say yes. 'Friendzone' is how we vilify a woman for exercising her right to say no.
29 April 2011
1 comment: **Nathan Hillary:** 'Fat' is how we vilify a woman for not exercising at all.

*

It's gonna be one of THOSE sorts of days thought Brad as the familiar first bars of the Star Wars theme song rang out.

"Turning it off," Brad said quickly, reaching into his pocket. "I'm turning it off." Within moments he had delivered on this promise.

"You're supposed to have cellphones turned off before you come into my class," said Dr. Johnson, reproachfully. Brad shrugged.

"No-one ever phones me," said Brad apologetically. "So I guess it slipped my mind."

"Honest answer," said Dr. Johnson. "Now please put that away, and I'll get back to the lesson."

*

When Brad turned his phone back on after the lecture, he found that he had missed calls from Evan, Seth and Kevin, along with an SMS from Evan, just saying 'Thor. Rosebank, 14:00'. Brad checked his watch. It was a quarter past one. Plenty of time to make it to Rosebank, as long as he managed to beat the lunch time rush out of

West. Brad quickly typed in a reply. 'Grab me a ticket, on my way.'

Brad pulled on the second shoulder strap of his backpack for more stability, and broke into a jog, heading toward the first-year parking lot at the bottom end of West Campus. He crossed the Amic deck well ahead of the crowds leaving from East Campus. If he could just get in front of the crowds on their way out of West Campus lecture venues, he'd be in the clear. He rounded the end of Amic deck and curved right. He had a straight run to the parking lot, but his path was lined with buildings full of lecture venues. Brad was dismayed to see a large crowd pour out of the doors of the New Commerce Building, right in his path.

Brad slowed to a brisk walk and started to weave through the crowd.

"Brad! Why the hurry?" came a voice just as he was breaking through into the open. It was Claudia, coming the opposite direction to Brad, walking up from the FNB building, the last lecture venue between Brad and the parking lot. Brad barely broke stride as he answered and Claudia fell into step with him.

"Need to get to my car ahead of the crowds! We're all gonna watch Thor at Rosebank." said Brad, angling for a gap through the last clump of students in his way.

"Does that mean WARP will be closed?" Claudia asked, sounding disappointed. "I guess I'll have to do something else with the afternoon."

"Come see Thor," suggested Brad, leading the way through the crowd. "I'll SMS Evan and have him get you a ticket."

*

By twenty to two, Rosebank Mall's lunchtime rush was well under way, and Brad was frantically searching for parking.

"Quick, round there," said Claudia, pointing to the left. "That guy in the Toyota looks like he's pulling out." Brad knew the parking spot wouldn't last long; in mere moments it would be spotted by one of its natural predators, a housewife in an SUV. Already accelerating, he spun the steering wheel to the left to swing toward the soon-to-be-vacant spot. Impatiently, Brad looked at his watch as he waited for the Toyota to make it out of the cramped parking bay.

Ten to two. The Toyota finally pulled away, and Brad started manoeuvring. He needed to get this right first time, and the parking spot was a tight fit. Biting his lip in concentration, Brad eased his way in.

"Eh, close enough," he said, pulling up the handbrake. "I'll have to follow you out the passenger door though." It was a short walk to the elevator, which, fortunately, went directly to the cinema complex. They found Evan waiting for them right outside the elevator, awkwardly holding two boxes of popcorn and two sodas.

"Everyone else is inside already," said Evan. "You should have told me you had company, I didn't get enough snacks. I assumed the second ticket was just you wouldn't have to sit next to a stranger." He turned to Claudia and handed her a box of popcorn. "Here," he said. "You can have Brad's. Come on, movie's about to start," he finished, leading the way to Cinema 1.

He led them to a row where Bernard, Seth and Kevin were sitting. The trailers were still running, but Bernard's popcorn was already finished and he was eying Kevin's. Seth had his Galaxy tablet out and was brushing up on Thor comic book trivia.

"Oh wow," said Bernard, pulling back in his chair to give them space to squeeze past. "We let Evan out of our sight for five minutes and he comes back with a girl."

"Actually, she came with Brad," said Evan. Bernard looked from Brad to Claudia and back again a few times, with a confused look on his face.

"That's Claudia," Kevin explained. "One of the WARP first years."

"She doesn't look like much of a geek," said Bernard sceptically.

"Well, she's only been in the club for a few months and she already knows how to play Magic," said Kevin.

"No she doesn't," said Seth, shaking his head.

*

"What was with all that sappy romantic stuff?" Bernard complained as they walked out of the cinema. "You don't go see a comic-book movie for generic romance. I want my money back!"

"You haven't paid me for your ticket," said Evan. Bernard paused.

"Um, yeah, about that. See, the thing is..." he started saying, but Evan interrupted him.

"Yeah, yeah," said Evan, rolling his eyes. "Pay me whenever you can, it's fine."

"I'm good for it," Bernard insisted. "I started that data capture job at Senate House; my first paycheck should clear any day now. No sign of Seth's character sheet though."

Behind Bernard, Seth and Kevin both went wide-eyed and pale. Evan glanced back at them and raised a finger to his lips.

"Adding in a bit of romance is pretty good business," said Evan. "Comic-book movies appeal to guys already, so the studio throws in a good-looking leading man and a romantic sub-plot and suddenly they've got a viable date movie. Makes for a much bigger audience."

"They really did skimp on fight scenes though," said Claudia. "As part of the female audience I can vouch that it's not enough for a guy to have muscles on screen, he needs to do something with them."

"Exactly!" said Bernard. "More fighting, less posing. Everyone agrees."

"For once, I'm glad they didn't stick to the comics," said Kevin. "It always seemed dumb to me, the idea that Thor was just a random human who transforms into a god."

"That's not strictly accurate," said Seth. "In the comics, Odin transfers Thor into Donald Blake's body to teach him humility, and removed his memories of being a god. It's not quite the typical scenario of an average person getting superpowers by accident."

"At least he wasn't bitten by a radioactive Norse God," said Evan.

*

"You'll have to direct me," said Brad. "I don't really know this area." It turned out that Claudia stayed near Rosebank, so Brad agreed to drop her off, and then take Kevin home as usual.

"Just carry on straight for now, I'll tell you when to turn left," replied Claudia. Traffic was normal for Joburg at that time of day, which is to say that it resembled Brownian Motion. Claudia was riding shotgun to direct Brad, and Kevin was sitting in the back.

"So what do you study?" Kevin asked, leaning forward.

"BA," Claudia said. "Majoring in linguistics."

"Interesting choice," said Kevin.

"I'm also doing a course in Mandarin at the West Language school," she continued. "I want to be a translator." Kevin and Brad both nodded, impressed. "How about you guys?" Claudia asked.

"I'm doing Electrical Engineering, second year," said Kevin. "Brad's in law, almost second year." Brad winced.

"So what got you into WARP?" Brad asked, changing the subject.

"I was recruited by Nathan," said Claudia. "He's crazy persuasive."

"Mostly just crazy," Brad corrected. "Do you want to guess why we don't keep food in the club-room fridge?" he asked. Claudia's brow furrowed as she starting imagining possibilities, and she started to look slightly ill.

"Dial back on the imagination there," said Brad. "It's nothing gross. He has the fridge positioned so that he can leave the door very slightly open without it being visible to people in the room. That means he can breathe while he waits for a good time to dramatically burst out."

"That is admirable commitment to a prank," Claudia commented.

"One time I saw him stay in there for almost an hour just to avoid talking to Tarryn," said Kevin.

"I guess she can be a bit preachy," said Claudia, shrugging. "Speaking of which," she added, looking thoughtful. "How did James ever get to be president? It's hard to imagine him winning an election."

"You know," said Brad. "I don't remember there even being an election last year."

"Actually," Kevin remarked. "I was cleaning out my spam folder the other day and I came across something about an election."

"How did WARP get tagged as spam?" asked Claudia.

"On purpose, I think," said Kevin. "The word 'enlargement' should never feature so prominently in an official communication."

"It sounds like James isn't too keen on high attendance at these things," said Claudia.

"He is pretty attached to that parking spot," remarked Brad.

Chapter 17

Jamie Rogers is now friends with **Claudia O'Reilly**
Jamie Rogers: Exams done and dusted. Holiday time!
        11 July 2011

*

Brad and Kevin walked into the club-room.

"Oh, hey guys," said James, quickly turning around and using his back to cover up what he had been writing on the whiteboard. "What brings you here during the holidays?"

"Here for the election," said Brad. The only people in the room with James were Seth and Bernard, who were sitting around the table looking bored.

"What?" said James, looking panicked. "How'd you know about the election?"

"I checked my spam folder,' said Brad. "Just to be clear, you did say there are absolutely no cheap iPhones or Viagra at this meeting? What about Nigerian fortunes you need help transferring out of the country?"

"I was saving that one for next year," James muttered. Kevin looked down to read a text on his phone.

"The rest are on their way," he said. "They're just grabbing coffee."

"The rest?" said James, worried.

"We were worried that your email might be tagged as spam for everyone in the club, so I passed the message along to a few people." James began to look nervous at the mention of more people coming.

"Just how many people?" he asked, with a calculating look on his face. Brad just smiled.

Claudia and Melvyn were the next to arrive, each carrying two cups of coffee.

"Here you go, Brad," said Claudia, handing one over. Kevin took the cup offered by Melvyn, along with two packets of sugar. Counting up the people in the room, James pulled out his phone and began hastily texting.

"Uh, does anyone have Nathan's actual number?" James asked. "I guess Ari will have to do," he said with a shrug when everyone shook their heads. He looked down at his phone and kept on texting.

"I know how you handled the emails," said Kevin, carefully pouring sugar into his coffee. "But tell me, James, how did you get around the SRC's requirement that you post the election date on the club notice-board?"

"Oh, it's posted," said James, briefly looking up from his phone. "It's there right now." Brad and Kevin both walked outside the door to peer at the notice-board. After a few moments of close inspection, Brad peeled back the corner of a Star Wars poster that was pinned to the board, revealing an official statement from the WARP executive committee about the election about to take place.

"I wonder how long that's been under there," said Tarryn, who had just walked up the corridor. "Thanks for the message, Brad," Tarryn continued. "It's about time WARP had a real election."

"It's good to see you," said Brad. "It's been a while."

"It has," she said. "Things were a bit awkward; I thought it'd be best if I spent some time away from all this." Brad shrugged.

"It was probably for the best," said Brad. "Welcome back. You didn't miss much."

"It's not at all awkward to be back," said Tarryn. "Looks like Evan just got here too," she continued, looking down the corridor.

"Hey Brad," said Evan, before exchanging polite greetings with Tarryn. Brad walked back into WARP and looked around the room.

"I guess it's about time we got this thing started," said Brad. "The notice said 11am."

"Ah, but we're allowed to wait up to thirty minutes if someone is delayed," said James. "I've got backup coming, assuming any of them get my message in time."

*

The half hour was almost up before a previous generation of WARPlings began to arrive. The first one through the door could almost pass as Seth's older brother; he was tall and thin, with pale skin and blue eyes. His dark hair was neatly trimmed and he was wearing a checked button-down shirt with suit trousers. Brad estimated him to be in his late 20s.

"Hi Daniel," said James. "Thanks for coming." The next arrival had light brown hair shaved almost down to the scalp. Thick muscular forearms showed that his bulk wasn't all fat, and he stood well over six feet tall. Thick stubble added to his intimidating appearance. "Fuzzy," said James, nodding his head in greeting. "Is anyone else coming?" he asked.

"Just Navish," answered Daniel. "JJ's in Cape Town, Kyle emigrated, and no-one else could get out of work."

"This had better be important," said Navish as he walked in through the door. "If you woke me up just to decorate Bernard again, we're gonna have a problem." Navish was of average build and a bit shorter than average height. He looked to be in his early 30s, and was wearing the WARP uniform of a black t-shirt with blue jeans.

"Relax," said Daniel. "Remember the time you called the cops on Adrian's brother?"

"Speaking of Nathan," said Navish. "Check the fridge." Brad had no idea that Nathan had an older brother who'd been in WARP, and it started to dawn on him that the club had a lot more history than he had realised.

"Clear," said Fuzzy, looking in the fridge.

"I like what you guys have done with the room, by the way," said Daniel.

"We've barely changed it since you graduated," said James, looking puzzled.

"Exactly," said Daniel. "Well, I have to get back to the office, how about we get this vote over with?"

"Ari should be here any moment," said James. "Though come to think of it, I'm not sure why I asked him to come. He's unpredictable. We might as well get started." As he said this, Ari walked in through the door.

"So that's Ari," said Daniel. "I've only ever talked to him on the phone."

"Same," said Navish. "He looks exactly how I pictured him."

"I don't know," said Daniel. "He didn't sound quite as hairy on the phone, and I thought he'd be taller." Ari's brow furrowed.

"I'm right here," he said, annoyed.

"Well spotted," said Daniel. "Very observant. Now let's vote already."

"Okay everybody," said James. "I hereby declare the opening of our annual executive committee election. Bernard, wake up. If anyone can remember what the official voting procedure is, please say so now." It was Daniel who answered.

"In principle we should start by voting on the position of president so that unsuccessful candidates can still stand for the other positions. In the interests of drama and narrative, however, let's start by electing the club secretary."

"I nominate Seth," said James. "He's the perfect choice, he's a spreadsheeting machine."

"Seconded," said Bernard. Everyone in the room seemed to agree with this, and no-one spoke up to make another nomination.

"Seth is elected unopposed," concluded Daniel. "Now for the position of treasurer."

"I nominate Tarryn," said Brad. "It'd do the club good to have someone level-headed running the finances."

"Seconded," said Kevin.

"I nominate Matt," said James.

"Seconded," said Bernard.

"He's not even here!" protested Brad.

"And I have no idea who that is," said Navish.

"Really?" said James. "Navish, he was here at the same time as you for like three years. Hell, he's been in half the DnD campaigns you've run since then." Navish just shook his head slowly.

"The rules say that candidates have to be present at the election," said Daniel.

"Really?" said James. "Huh. Well, against my better judgment, I nominate Bernard."

"Bernard? Are you crazy?" said Navish. "Tarryn it is," he continued, and a flurry of hands shot up to vote for Tarryn.

"Now for the big one," said Daniel. "Who are our nominees for the position of president?"

"I nominate James for president," said Seth, sounding bored.

"Seconded," said Bernard.

"I nominate Evan," said Brad.

"I refuse," said Evan, quickly. "Too much work. I nominate Brad," he said, much to Brad's surprise.

"Seconded," said Tarryn.

"I'm not sure I'm a suitable candidate," Brad protested. "This is only my second year here, I don't know if I'd be up to it."

"This is for next year's exec, so you'll be a third-year by then," Evan explained. And you'll have to be doing a second-year subject anyway, so you can go light on your course-load without delaying your graduation. That means plenty of free time."

"It seems we have two candidates," said Daniel. "All voting for James as president, raise your hands," he finished, raising his own hand.

There were five hands raised, Bernard, Seth, Navish and Fuzzy added their votes to Daniel's.

"All in favour of this newbie for president," Daniel continued, pointing to Brad. "Please raise your hands."

This time there were six hands raised. Brad was stunned but happy. Things were a bit of a blur, but he remembered Kevin patting him on the back and Evan high-fiving him.

"It seems we have a tie," Daniel was saying. "Bernard, you can't vote twice."

"My bad," said Bernard, lowering his hand.

"Ari, you didn't vote," said Daniel. "It seems the deciding vote is yours." Ari shrugged.

"I've never actually signed up for WARP," he said. "You people just keep phoning me."

"I haven't voted yet," said Nathan, bursting out of the fridge.

"I thought you said it was clear," said Daniel.

"I didn't want to ruin it for him," said Fuzzy, shrugging.

"Someone get me a jacket," said Nathan, shivering "I think I might have hypothermia." Wordlessly, Brad handed him the jacket he'd brought with him.

"Thanks Brad," said Nathan. "You're president."

Chapter 18

Jamie Rogers: I am flattered and honoured to have been elected president of WARP. Guys, I will do my best to live up to the trust you have placed in me
18 July 2011

*

"Mom, Dad, I have some news," said Brad. They were sitting together at the dinner table, settling into a healthy meal of roast beef and steamed vegetables. Jarryd was already finished, and was fidgeting and eying the fridge.

"I knew this day would come," said Jarryd, turning to look towards their parents. "See? What did I tell you?"

"It's okay, Jamie," said his mom. "You can tell us anything." Brad's brow furrowed in confusion, but he kept going.

"I won't ask what news you're expecting," said Brad. "I was going to tell you that I have been elected the president of WARP."

"That's actually worse," said Jarryd thoughtfully.

"That's wonderful," said his mom.

"I still don't know what WARP is," said his dad.

"It means that Jamie is now King of the Nerds," Jarryd explained.

"As long as it's what makes you happy, we support you," said Brad's dad.

"I hope no-one at school hears about this," said Jarryd. "It was bad enough when his brass band was in the newspaper."

"This is excellent news," said Brad's mom. "It's a big deal to be president of a student club. According to the SRC website," said his mom, browsing on her phone. "WARP has 180 members, and all club members have to be invited to elections. That's a lot of people voting for our boy." Brad flushed slightly as he remembered how the elections really went, and he resolved that as president he would make sure WARP got a proper election.

"Wait," said Jarryd. "So this means he's popular? That's incredible. We should get pizza to celebrate." Brad paused as he was lowering his fork to his food, and stared at Jarryd in disbelief. Jarryd shrugged, unembarrassed.

"I'm still hungry, okay?"

"There's some leftover beef in the fridge," said Brad's mom. "Jarryd, you can go make yourself a sandwich, you're excused from the table."

"Yes!" said Jarryd, pumping a fist in excitement.

*

"Does WARP really have a hundred and eighty members?" Brad asked. He was in the club-room along with Tarryn for their weekly briefing from the incumbent members of the executive. The newly elected committee would only assume their positions at the start of the next year, but it was traditional to involve them in day-to-day proceedings as soon as they were elected. The meeting was fairly small; Seth was returning as secretary and Matt was absent. James had explained that Matt's position had been nominal; no-one had ever told him that he held it.

"One hundred and seventy eight members, to be exact," said Seth. "O-week recruiting was highly successful this year. We also bumped up the membership fee, so our budget is huge."

"What are you going to do with it?" Tarryn asked.

"Fish-tank!" yelled Melvyn. "Stripper Pole!" he added.

"Pick one dumb idea and stick with it," said James.

"Melvyn, why are you even here?" asked Tarryn.

"To make sure WARP gets the stripper tank it needs!" said Melvyn.

"Moving swiftly along," said James. "We're thinking a set of new couches and a PC for the club-room." Brad did some quick mental arithmetic, based on the membership fee he remembered paying.

"That still leaves a lot of money left over," he said. "Does the budget roll over each year?"

"It does," said James. "But there won't be anything left over. We can only spend club money buying from West-designated vendors and they're all hilariously overpriced. Presumably, someone in management gets a kickback."

"Surely the SRC would support us in finding our own suppliers to stretch our budget?" said Brad, taken aback by the blasé discussion of such unethical behaviour. "They're all about improving student life, aren't they?" he asked. James sighed.

"Don't be so naive, Brad," said James, shaking his head ruefully. "The SRC has only two goals: Pocketing bribes and avoiding work. They don't get to do much of the first because they have no real power, so they mostly stick to the second. Clubs create work for them, so as far as they're concerned our existence is a problem. Someone higher up gets to skim our budgets, that's the only reason they don't let the SRC shut down every club they can." Brad was appalled, and it clearly showed on his face, because James's voice turned sympathetic.

"This university is a monument to apathy," said James. "And yeah, most of the people who seem to care are just trying to embezzle, but here at WARP we have a good thing. The committee's job is to keep everyone happy enough to let the club keep existing. If we manage to get a few couches and a computer on top of that, that's just a bonus."

*

"Regardless of what James says," said Brad. "I think we can make a real difference to the people in this club." Brad was sitting with Tarryn and Seth in the club-room, brainstorming ideas for their tenure on the committee. James's meeting had lasted barely five minutes; in fact he had left shortly after his monologue.

"This current executive is useless," Brad continued. "But that doesn't mean we have to follow their footsteps into mediocrity."

"I'm still in the room," said Seth.

"Exactly," sa`id Tarryn. "They did nothing the year before that and then re-elected themselves just to do nothing once again. The longer they stayed there, the worse they got."

"Club secretary three years running," said Seth. "And right here in the room with you."

"This year is going to be different," said Brad, standing up and walking over to the whiteboard. "WARP needs to move with the times. It needs new ideas. Fresh faces."

"If it's okay with you guys," said Seth. "I'll go on using my old spreadsheets as a template."

"What WARP needs," said Brad, picking up a whiteboard marker and drawing flow diagrams freehand. "Is a bigger online footprint."

"We could have our own website," suggested Tarryn. "Where we can inform members about events and keep everybody in touch."

"That's a great idea," said Brad. "We can use the clubroom computer as a server; it'll be permanently connected to the West network. Seth can set it all up."

"Has Seth agreed to all this?" asked Seth. "It sounds like a lot of work to just dump on the guy."

"We could also set up a Facebook group and maybe a Twitter account," said Tarryn. "We can have polls on Facebook when we have big decisions to make," she suggested. "That way we can run this club democratically."

"As long as everyone's voice is heard," said Seth sarcastically while Brad nodded agreement with Tarryn.

Chapter 19

Nathan Hillary: Blink and you'll miss it. If you don't blink your eyes dry up and fall out. There's no winning.
22 August 2011

*

"Are there any pictures of Nathan where he's smiling?" Claudia asked.

"One," said Kevin. "In the dictionary under 'autism'."

It was the first day of the second semester, and the club-room was relatively crowded. Brad was one of a small group sitting at the new club-room PC, building a Facebook profile for WARP.

"What about Bernard?" said Claudia. "I bet he gets up to some interesting stuff."

"Yeah," said Kevin dubiously. "But nothing we'd want the world to see. Tarryn wanted us to promote the club, not drive people away."

"WARPlings hate being photographed," said Seth. "I don't think that there's much you can use."

"You could at least try to help," said Claudia. "You said you have a whole hard-drive of pictures, there must be something we can use."

"Those are just memes I've archived over the years," said Seth. "When I suggested a clubroom PC I was thinking along the lines of editing Tvtropes.org and trolling Reddit. Not saturating social media."

"How about those old photo albums James gave us on his flash drive," asked Claudia. "There must be something we can use in there."

"Opening it up now," said Kevin. "Which folder should we check out first? 'LARP and New Years' sounds pretty boring. 'Possible Felony' sounds ominous. 'Pillow fight 2009' can't be too bad, I say we check that."

"Possible Felony," Claudia replied without hesitation. Reluctantly, Kevin moved his cursor to the folder. At that moment, the club-room door swung open, and Evan stepped through.

"Nathan's up to something downstairs," said Evan. "It'll be worth seeing."

"But downstairs is far," said Bernard grumpily.

"Ah, but it's also down," said Evan. "Gravity will be on your side for once." Bernard brightened up, failing to think as far ahead as the journey back.

*

The group followed Evan downstairs and outside the Matrix. A large crowd had gathered there, moderately interested in a promotional contest happening on a stage that had been set up in the middle of the lawn. In the centre of the stage was a ball pit, filled mostly with blue plastic balls. As the group wove their way to the front of the audience, a blindfolded contestant was in the pit, scrabbling through the balls and listening to instructions from the crowd, trying to find the white balls that were interspersed amongst the blue ones.

"This had better be good," said James as he joined the group. "I was at home when you texted me."

"You got here just in time," said Evan. "Nathan's up next."

"Is that all we came here for?" said Claudia. "Watching Nathan do some dumb contest?" Brad shrugged.

"Even if it seems dumb, we geeks should support each other," he said. "Though I must admit this doesn't seem like Nathan's sort of thing."

"Actually I'm with Claudia on this," said Evan. "If I hadn't seen Nathan buying effervescent tablets in the 7/11, I wouldn't come within a mile of this junk." As he was saying this, Nathan was being blindfolded and led to the ball pit. The crowd joined in with the countdown, and Nathan composed himself for a massive effort. As he heard the command to go, he dropped to his knees and began scrabbling.

A few seconds later, he collapsed flat on his face, thrashing fitfully as foam sprayed from his mouth. The contest organisers froze for a moment, trying to decide whether minimum wage was worth this level of trouble. They fled in every direction.

Evan leaped onto the stage and turned Nathan onto his side, before he collapsed beside him and joined in his efforts, foam spraying from his mouth as his long hair whipped around. "It's contagious!" yelled Seth, scattering the crowd while Melvyn leaped onto the stage and helped himself to the unattended prizes.

*

"Who wears this crap?" said Melvyn, throwing a pair of skinny jeans onto the table in disgust. They were back in the club-room and Brad was eating his lunch while watching Melvyn appraise his haul of loot. Claudia was back at the WARP PC, logging back into the WARP Facebook account and plugging her phone in by USB.

"I tried these on," said Nathan, eying a pair of jeans disdainfully. "But it was like trying to stick my leg into a condom."

"How are so many hipsters able to fit into these?" asked Evan. "Surely there aren't that many surgeons willing to surgically remove a guy's calves?"

"Maybe it's a line of clothing for guys who thought the term 'food allergy' applies to all food in general," suggested Nathan.

"Well, I think I got WARP's new profile photo," Claudia announced abruptly from where she was sitting.

"Claudia, no," protested Evan as he turned around to get a good look at what was on the monitor. "That's not just embarrassing, it's incriminating. Melvyn is actively stealing in the background."

"You can't see his face, it wouldn't hold up as evidence", Claudia argued. "And Nathan isn't doing anything illegal, he's just flailing around with a memorable facial expression. Besides," she continued. "I've already posted it."

"We can just change it back after you leave," said Evan. "So you might as well save us the effort."

"Or," she said. "I can change the account password and just be on my way. See you later!" she said cheerfully as she left the room.

"So how does it feel to be the face of WARP?" Evan asked Nathan. "The crazed, contorted face, that is," he added. Nathan just shrugged.

"Seth has a keystroke logger on this PC," said Nathan. "I can find out what she changed the password to any time. Not to mention, she logged onto her own Facebook account earlier."

"Aw yeah!" said Melvyn. "Someone's getting some embarrassing posts on her timeline!"

"Not exactly," said Nathan. "Someone's birthday is just getting set to invisible without her realising."

"Wow," said Melvyn with wonder in his voice. "That is true evil."

"And if you've ever wondered why Tarryn gets depressed around July," Nathan added. "Now you know."

Chapter 20

Jamie "Bradford" Rogers: Passed all my subjects! 2012 is gonna be a great year.
16 January 2012

*

It was a blisteringly hot Highveld Summer's day. It was only midmorning and already the glaring sun made Brad glad that being club president gave him shaded parking directly beneath the Matrix, where he'd have only a short walk to the club-room.

"Perks of the job, huh?" Kevin commented as Brad parked.

"Walking from First-Year parking isn't much shorter than walking from home," said Brad. "I can see why James held onto the position so tightly."

It was a Monday and time for the new WARP executive's first meeting with the SRC. But Brad's first order of business was collecting his club-room key from campus security.

"Hi there," he said, sliding his paperwork and student card into the tray under the window at the security office counter. "Collecting my key." His documents, stamped and signed by the Dean of Student Affairs, gave his name and student number and stated that he had been appointed the president of War-Games and Roleplay.

"War-games, huh?" said the security officer, selecting from a rack of keys up on the wall. "Down by Science Stadium, right?"

"WARP," Brad corrected. "In the Matrix."

"Right, right," said the security officer, taking a different key. He ticked off a register and then slid the key back to Brad along with his paperwork and student card.

"What was that about another club called War-Games?" Kevin asked as they started on their way to the Matrix.

"No idea," said Brad. "I guess I'll ask James when I get a chance."

With the university still on holiday, the queue for coffee at Nino's was blissfully short so Brad and Kevin were soon on their way to the clubroom with coffee in hand. Brad paused a moment in the door, looking around the clubroom that had become like a second home.

Bernard was napping on the couch while Seth and Tarryn sat at the clubroom PC, logged on to manage the WARP Facebook group. Nathan had his feet up on the table, leaning back in an office chair looking bored. James was standing behind Seth and Tarryn, looking disapproving.

"Weird thing happened when I was collecting my room key," said Brad. "The guy at the counter seemed to get us confused with another club called War-Games. What's that about?"

"Oh, that," said James, waving a hand dismissively. "War-Games is an old club, totally separate from us. We're a social club, falling under the SRC. They're a sports club, falling under the Sports Council. These days they don't have the minimum membership for an active club."

"One more year and they get dissolved permanently," added Seth, looking round from the clubroom pc. "We used to compete with them for membership, until we perfected recruiting and buried them."

"Hey, remember the time they tried to use our budget by just claiming they were us?" said James, laughing.

"With the names so similar they'd have gotten away with it," said Seth. "If Nathan hadn't been spying on them."

"Yeah, yeah," said Nathan. "Go me. Now can we get on with the meeting?"

"Happy New Year to you too," said Kevin. "How is everyone doing?" he asked, looking around the room with a smile.

"Yeah," added James. "Who failed what, and how bad?"

"I passed everything," said Brad. "But I didn't get to take many third-year courses, so I have a pretty open timetable."

"Regrettably, I am now split-course," said Kevin. "I'm repeating Signals and Systems from second-year. There're a bunch of third-year courses that it's a prerequisite for so I've ended up with a lot of free time too,"

"Don't worry about it," said Seth. "Hardly anyone passes engineering without repeating a year here and there. It happens to the best of us."

"No it doesn't," said Nathan. "How about you, Seth? You get into fourth-year this time around?"

"I did indeed," said Seth. "If everything goes smoothly I'll be done this year."

"I passed everything," said Tarryn. "I need to put in some work this year though, to get into Honours." Nathan raised an eyebrow at her.

"Honours?" he said. "So this is still your first degree, and you've been here how many years?"

"For some of us, university offers more than just academics.," replied Tarryn, waving a finger. "It's about social maturation and personal growth."

"I grew an inch taller when I was a first-year," said Nathan. "Does that count? Besides, I'm not advocating high attendance or anything like that. I just say that if you're going to show up for a test anyway, you might as well put down answers that are right."

"Great system, Nathan. Revolutionary stuff," said Brad. "Now if you're done being a jerk, let's move onto discussing O-Week."

"He'll be a jerk about that too," Seth pointed out.

"He's not wrong," said Nathan, shrugging. "But I've got a nice efficient strategy this year. I call it Only Monday Matters, or OMM for short."
"Oh yeah?" said Brad. "And what does it entail?"

"Simple," said Nathan. "We always get most of our recruitments on Monday, before people get desensitised. They're much more susceptible to recruitment."

"It's true," said Seth. "I ran the numbers."

"And the earlier we sign someone up," Nathan added. "The more time they have to talk their friends into signing up too. So recruitments are both easier and more valuable early in the week."

"I ran those numbers too," said Seth. "His theory checks out."

"There you go," said Nathan. "So let's just have an all-out blitz on the Monday and then can relax for the rest of the week."

"I don't know," said Brad. "I mean, what if it doesn't work out? The logic seems solid, but I don't want to risk our whole recruitment drive on it."

"What's to risk?" said Nathan. "If it doesn't work out, we'll know by Monday afternoon. Then you just keep working at it the rest of the week and there's no harm done."

"I actually think it's a good idea," said Tarryn. "We can make a big effort on the Monday and keep a skeleton crew at the stall after that. Nathan's our most successful recruiter, so I guess we put him at the stall all day on Monday, and rotate who goes with him."

"Send Brad," said Nathan. "We have a good dynamic where I'm harsh and abrasive to him. His willingness to put up with it makes him seem worldly and interesting. Biggest con in the world, but it makes it seem like we're a club of interesting people."

"I like the plan," said Kevin. "If it pays off we can hit the O-Week parties without worrying about hangovers affecting our recruiting skills."

Brad felt a bit irritated. He'd been thinking up recruitment plans for weeks. He'd already mocked up some flyers at home and was working on a design for a banner. It was almost time for the meeting with the SRC, and he hadn't even gotten a chance to mention his ideas yet. As president, he'd figured people would at least listen to him on club matters.

"I was thinking," said Brad, keeping his annoyance out of his voice to sound reasonable. "That we could do some more advertising of the club. Maybe hang up a banner, hand out flyers." Nathan shrugged.

"Handing out flyers at West is basically littering," he said. "But we have a big portrait of Leonard Nimoy that we could put up."

"Sounds logical," said Seth. "I guess that's about it for O-Week planning. And just in time too, we have to get to the SRC offices."

*

"I think this is the worst thing that has happened in all of history," said Seth. "And I'm Jewish."

Dejected, WARP's executive committee walked slowly down the corridor outside the SRC office. The meeting had been a short one, but devastating.

"Maybe the new room won't be so bad," said Brad, not managing much sincerity. "They did promise that it would be at least the same size and with equivalent fittings."

"That's not the point," said Seth, shaking his head. "The DJ Du Plessis building is FAR, Brad. No-one will walk all the way to the other end of West Campus just to hang out in between classes."

"I'm sure it's not so bad," said Tarryn. "It will take some getting used to but we'll make the best of it." Seth looked dubious. As they walked together into WARP, he pulled out his laptop as Brad slumped onto a couch.

Brad couldn't believe that within his first month as president, WARP had lost the club-room. This hammer blow to the club had been innocuously labelled 'Office re-allocations' by the SRC.

"According to Google Maps, it's a 1.6km walk from Central Block to the DJ Du Plessis building," said Seth. "That's fifteen to twenty minutes each way. Bernard skips too many classes as it is, imagine if he has to walk a mile each way every time he goes to one."

"So when do we break the news to everyone?" said Brad. "I'd prefer to do it after O-week, I don't want everyone too depressed to recruit."

"They said we only have to actually move in May," said Tarryn. "So I guess we can wait a while. On the other hand, the sooner everyone knows, the more time we'll have to plan for the move and figure out how to keep the club together."

"If the OMM philosophy proves solid we can announce it on the Tuesday of O-Week," said Seth. "That way the main recruitment still happens but we maximise our planning time."

"We can do that," said Brad. "But only if our recruitment on Monday is as good as we expect."

*

Chapter 21

Bernard Cronje: I just got a piece of dental floss stuck in my teeth. I have never felt so betrayed.
25 January 2012

*

The fateful meeting with the SRC had left Brad brooding and despondent. Two days later he was home alone with Jarryd, their parents being out at a St John's staff dinner. Unable to summon the motivation to do anything but mope around the house, Brad lay on the couch with his 3DS, disinterestedly grinding levels in Pokemon.

"What say we go get pizza?" said Jarryd, nudging him in the ribs. "Mom and dad left us money for food."

"I'm watching my weight," said Brad, patting his belly. In truth, it jiggled far less than it used to.

"Come on," Jarryd insisted. "Cheat meals help with fat-burning. Raises leptin bro." Brad looked at him askance.

"Where'd you even learn that word?" Brad asked.

"My rowing coach has been teaching us about diet," Jarryd explained. "He says that insulin sensitivity is the key, not counting calories. I'll explain it all over pizza."

"Fine," said Brad, putting down his 3DS with a sigh. "Let's go get pizza." Depressingly, his decision to leave the couch had a lot to do with having lost three battles in a row.

*

It was a half hour drive to Gino's, but their pizza made it worthwhile. Brad had been coming to the restaurant with his parents for as long as he could remember. After thirty years of booming business, Gino's was still a family restaurant, and it was Gino himself who greeted them at the door.

"Table for four?" the slim, gray-haired Italian asked as Brad and Jarryd walked through the heavy wooden doors.

"Just two, Gino. My parents are out for the night."

"I see," said Gino. "I'll seat you close to the kitchen so Jarryd doesn't have to wait long for his pizza." Brad had been coming to the restaurant long enough to be familiar with most of the staff, so he was surprised that their waitress wasn't anyone he recognized. She was also cute enough to set Brad's palms sweating. Taller than average with an athletic build and long dark hair, she was pale with a smattering of light freckles.

"I'm Karen, and I'll be your waitress tonight," she said. Brad peered down at his menu as he thought through possible responses.

"I'm Brad, and I'll be your customer tonight," was the first thing that came to mind. *No,* he thought, *that's a dad joke, very corny. I need something better.* Brad hadn't yet come up with anything when Jarryd spoke up.

"I'm Jarryd," said Jarryd. "And I'll be your customer tonight," he finished, bringing a wince from Brad.

"Where did that dad joke come from?" said Brad. "You don't even have a girlfriend, never mind kids." Jarryd gave him a flat look, while Karen laughed.

"Don't mind him," said Brad. "And don't serve him alcohol, he's only seventeen."

"Thanks Jamie," said Jarryd. "World's greatest wingman over here. I guess I'll have a virgin chocolate milkshake, then."

"I'll have a coffee," said Brad. Brad found himself watching as Karen walked away. With a start, he averted his eyes, only to see that Jarryd was eying her just as avidly.

"Take a picture," said Brad. "It'll last longer."

"Bad idea," said Jarryd, shaking his head. "That's technically harassment. I thought you were studying law, you should know these things."

"I wasn't being serious," said Brad. "I was just pointing out that it's rude to stare."

"You were doing it too," Jarryd pointed out.

"Just pick a pizza, Jarryd."

"I think I'm gonna make a run on her when she gets back," said Jarryd. "Wingman me."

"Leave it until after we've eaten," said Brad. "That way it doesn't ruin our meal if it goes bad. Not to mention she looks a little old for you."

"She's eighteen, tops," said Jarryd. "Girls start putting on weight after high school."

"That's a generalization," said Brad. "And kind of a gross one."

"Whatever," said Jarryd. "We'll ask her after eating. If she's eighteen or less, I'll ask her out. If she's nineteen and up, you ask her out."

"I don't think we get to divide girls up like that," said Brad.

"Don't be an idiot," said Jarryd. "We aren't selling her. It just makes a bit more sense to match up ages."

"I still don't like it," said Brad.

"Fine," said Jarryd. "Then it's every man for himself. I'm warning you; I'll have no mercy."

"Fine," said Brad. "When the pizza's are finished, the gloves come off."

*

With only a few slices left of his pizza, Brad excused himself to go to the bathroom.

"It's true what they say," he said to Jarryd as he was standing up. "You don't buy coffee, you just rent it."

Brad spent a few minutes touching up his hair in front of the bathroom mirror and trying to compose himself, realising that with both he and Jarryd trying to shoot each other down it was more than likely that neither of them would succeed. Brad was thinking through ways to shut Jarryd down when he suddenly remembered something Nathan had said in the meeting earlier in the week. Jarryd being abrasive could actually play into his hands, as long as he could play it off lightly. With a nod, Brad set off back to the table. As he got close, he discovered that Jarryd had exploited the rules they'd laid down by finishing off Brad's pizza and calling Karen over to the table.

"My brother's a giant nerd," Jarryd was saying. "He has more Pokemon than he has friends."

"In my defense," said Brad, taking his seat. "I have a lot of Pokemon. Excuse my brother's rudeness, he was raised in a barn." Karen chuckled at that.

"Is it true about the Pokemon, though?" she asked.

"Not sure," said Brad. "Though I do check my Pokedex more often than my Facebook."

"Jamie's chief nerd at the West War-Games club," Jarryd added. His tactics didn't seem to be working too well, but he was a man to stick to his guns. Karen looked surprised.

"Oh, that's pretty cool," she said, smiling. "I've heard of the War-Games club." The conversation was going well for Brad, so he didn't want to bog it down by explaining the differences between WARP and War-Games.

"So I guess we're famous, then," he said with a grin.

"War-Games has that club-room by the Science Stadium, right?" she asked.

"Yeah," said Brad, reaching for the bill. "That's us." He studied the bill, trying to decide on an appropriate tip. Too much would seem desperate and creepy, but too little would definitely not impress her. It was a delicate balance, and Brad was giving it the careful thought it required. He resolved to go higher than the customary ten percent.

"Will you be running a bar for the Sports Council party in O-Week?" Karen asked, excited.

"Uh..." said Brad, starting to feel like the conversation was getting away from him. Tipping fifteen percent made the total a nice round number, which made the large amount seem more innocuous.

"What am I even saying?" said Karen, rolling her eyes. "Every sports club runs a bar, it's O-Week's biggest party. No need to write your phone number on that bill, I'll be seeing you next week! I'm in the rowing club, our room is right next to yours."

"That's awesome," said Brad. "I'll see you there!"

*

"That looked like it went well for you," said Jarryd on the ride home. "But something doesn't seem quite right about it."

"You don't say," said Brad.

"I don't just mean that we forgot to get an extra pizza to take home," said Jarryd. "Something else. I just can't quite put my finger on it."

"Do I really need to spell it out?" Brad asked.

"You read all my report cards," said Jarryd. "What do you think?"

"When you put it that way," said Brad. "I guess I'll say it slowly and clearly. I'm not president of War-Games, Jarryd. I'm president of WARP, it's a different club entirely. One without a club-room by Science Stadium."

"I see where you're going with this," said Jarryd, nodding. "You're saying I still have a shot."

*

The next morning, Brad parked under the Matrix and made his way to Campus Security in Central Block. He walked past the counter once, glancing to confirm that the security officer on duty wasn't the same one who had issued him his WARP key the previous week. Brad first went to a bathroom before circling back around, to avoid looking suspicious to anyone paying attention.

"Here to collect my key," said Brad, once again sliding his paperwork and student card through the slot at the counter. "War-Games, over by Science Stadium," he continued, mostly managing to keep his nerves out of his voice.

"Here you go," said the security officer after glancing at Brad's paperwork and selecting a key from the rack. "Looks like this one hasn't been used in a while," he added as he slid it through the slot where Brad picked it up.

The Science Stadium was just the other side of the Amic deck. Originally an athletics stadium, it had been rebuilt to house brand new chemistry labs and lecture venues. The stadium shape had been retained, replacing the track with an open quad. Around the back of the stadium, the sports clubs were found, fronting onto the road that looped around the stadium.

Brad drove along the road, looking up at the signs as he searched for War-Games. Sure enough, he found it right next to the rowing club. The room had a wide facade with two gray double doors, and plenty of space for Brad to park right in front.

"Here goes nothing," Brad said to himself, pulling out his new key and trying it in the door on the right. When it didn't fit, he moved to the door on the left and tried it there. After a few moments of fiddling with it, the lock clicked, and Brad pulled open the door.

The room inside was easily twice the size of WARP, but it was sparsely furnished and coated in fine dust. There were two couches in the middle of the room, thankfully covered with sheets. In the back corner were a sink and two fridges. Brad walked in and, with a smile, jokingly checked both fridges, just in case. There was also a store-room that opened out from one side of the room, but Brad had no key for the heavy padlock on its security gate.

Brad looked around to survey the room that was, for the moment, effectively his. There were no windows, the floors were bare concrete and the walls were rough brick with flaking white paint.

All-in-all, it looked like a disused bomb shelter.

Chapter 22

Nathan Hillary: To the uninitiated, any sufficiently complicated theory is indistinguishable from bullshit.
4 February 2011

*

"Pardon me, can I have just twenty seconds of your time?" said Nathan. It was the Monday of O-Week, and Brad was taking the morning shift alongside Nathan. Brad had never seen Nathan so polite during recruiting. Or ever.

"Sure thing," said the person Nathan had addressed, a brunette girl obviously in first-year based on all the O-Week maps and schedules she was carrying.

"Thanks," said Nathan peering down at his watch and pressing a button to start the stopwatch function. After twenty seconds of awkward silence, Nathan looked back up. "Thank you," he said, turning to look around for other people to recruit. The girl just stood there looking confused, eventually looking toward Brad questioningly. He gestured for her to walk to his end of the stall.

"Don't mind Nathan," said Brad. "Between you and me, he is several sandwiches short of a single sandwich." A few minutes of casual conversation persuaded the girl to sign up and revealed that she was an engineering student and that her name was Jess.

"Nicely done Brad," said Nathan. "As a reward, I'll actually give you enough money when I send you to get me coffee."

"Here I thought being president would mean I wouldn't be sent for the coffee anymore," Brad complained.

"If you read the WARP constitution very carefully," said Nathan. "You'll find that your actual title is 'Guy tricked into work'."

"I think I just might amend that clause," said Brad.

"You probably should," said Nathan, nodding. "The wording is sexist. Hi," he said to another girl walking past the stall. "It's gullible awareness week and we're collecting donations."

*

"How was the first session of recruiting?" Kevin asked as Brad walked into the club-room.

"Going well so far," said Brad. "It's at least thirty," he added.

"I'm sure Seth will be happy to count them up," said Kevin, gesturing to where Seth was sitting at his laptop.

"Counting by hand is a waste of time," said Seth, picking up his backpack and putting it on the table next to his laptop. "I've come up with something more efficient," he continued, using both hands to carefully slide a cardboard box out of one of his backpack's partitions. Opening the box, he started lifting out the parts of a triple beam balance. "There should be very little variance in the weight of signup sheets. All I need to do is figure out the average weight and then I'll be able to count a whole pile just by weighing it."

"I'm not sure that can be described as time saving, exactly," said Kevin. "Might be a little bit of the opposite."

"Done!" Seth announced proudly.

"So how many is it?" Brad asked, looking over at Seth, who stared back at him blankly for a few moments.

"I meant that I'm done assembling the scale," said Seth. "Now to calibrate."

"There are forty two signups," said Kevin. "I just picked them up and counted them." Seth ignored him and carried on with what he was doing. "It's a pretty impressive number for one session," Kevin added. "This Only Monday Matters strategy might just work after all."

"Seems like it," said Brad. "Another couple of sessions like that and we'll be half-way to hitting record membership."

"So who's at the stall right now?" Kevin asked, while Seth continued to tinker with the scale.

"Melvyn and James," Brad answered, settling down on the couch.

"You sure those two will be fine?" Kevin asked. "James is kind of a jerk, and Melvyn's unpredictable."

"Those are good points," said Brad. "Let's grab lunch and then we can swing by the stall and see how they're doing."

"By my calculations," said Seth. "There are forty one point six signup sheets here."

*

Brad approached the stall tentatively. A heated argument was underway and Brad could sense the tension.

"Does plausible deniability mean nothing to you?" James was demanding. "Those people will show up at the club-room expecting an ice-cream bar and a stripper pole, Melvyn."

"I do things my way," Melvyn protested, smacking a fist into the table, scattering a bunch of Warhammer Figurines. "I might not work by the book, but I get results!"

"We've got the SRC on our backs about member complaints and here you are promising X-Box and sushi on Thursday nights! You're a loose cannon, Melvyn. Turn in your clipboard and badge, NOW. And I don't want you going anywhere near recruitment. You're off the job."

Apprehensive, Brad stepped up to the stall.

"Hi guys," he said, tentatively. "How's recruitment going?" he asked.

"Pretty well," said Melvyn. "I've really gotten the hang of it."

"We're way past our goals for the day so now we're just doing movie spoofs," said James. "You should have seen Melvyn's Godzilla."

"How many have we signed up?" Brad asked.

"Haven't counted up," James said. "But it's a hefty stack. Probably twenty-five or thirty for the session." Meanwhile, Melvyn was theatrically waving his arms and throwing rapid-fire punches in the open air.

"You recruited my father," he said, pointing to a passer-by and moving his lips rapidly, out of sync with the words. But my Kung-Fu is strong. Now I will recruit you!" he finished, brandishing a signup sheet and pen.

*

On Tuesday morning The Matrix was bustling with crowds, as it often was during O-Week. Brad eyed the lengthy queue in Nino's, and considered heading upstairs without getting coffee.

"Tell you what," Kevin said over the noise of the crowd. "I'll get the coffee and meet you upstairs. You don't want to be late for your own meeting."

Nodding gratefully, Brad turned and headed for the club-room. By the time he arrived, Seth had already opened the room and was sitting at the clubroom PC, entering details from signup sheets. At one side of the table, James and Evan were playing a game of Magic while Bernard ate a breakfast of scrambled eggs and ham at the other end. Tarryn was sitting on a couch talking to Claudia. Ari and Melvyn were at the bookshelf, leafing through some of the manga there.

"Let's get this meeting going," said Melvyn, turning around as Brad walked in. "We've got recruiting to do!"

"I'm having a good hair day," added Ari, rubbing his chin, which was covered in what could only be called 'shaved before breakfast, not after' shadow. "So I want to get to the stall to scope out some first years."

"Kevin's downstairs on official business," Brad announced. "He'll be with us momentarily, and then we'll start the meeting. In the meantime, let's review our Monday recruiting. Seth, what were our final numbers?"

"One hundred and eight," said Seth. "That's a single-day recruitment record. Thirty eight of them are girls, which is well above our normal percentage."

"Big-ups for diversity!" shouted Melvyn, high-fiving Ari.

"Yeah," said Ari shiftily. "Diversity." At that moment Kevin walked in.

"What are we celebrating?" he asked, eying Melvyn and Ari. "Here's your coffee, by the way," he finished, handing the cup to Brad.

"Big recruiting day yesterday," Brad explained. "Now that everyone is here," he continued, taking a deep breath to steady his nerves. "I'm afraid I have some bad news. There's no easy way to say this, so I'll be blunt. We lost the club-room."

A hush fell over the room. Most of WARP stared blankly as they processed the news.

"Where did you see it last?" asked Melvyn. "If we retrace your steps I'm sure it'll turn up." Everyone just ignored him and after waiting a few moments for the news to sink in, Brad went on.

"The SRC did club-room reallocations. They've moved us to a room in the DJ Du Plessis building."

"Oh God," said Kevin. "That's in the bottom corner of West Campus. It's quicker to go home than to walk that far."

"They can't kick us out," said Bernard. "I have squatter's rights."

"Technically correct," said James. "Bernard sleeps here often enough that the university can't forcibly evict him."

"Problem solved," said Bernard, leaning back smugly.

"However," James continued. "They could just change the locks when you go outside to use the bathroom. And I'm pretty sure that squatting in a university building would be good enough grounds for the university to expel you." Bernard slumped in his seat, and the room was silent once again.

"What if the room is declared unfit for human habitation?" asked Kevin. "Then they can't hand it over to anyone else."

"If it's not habitable it's not much use for us, either," said James. "So that's not the best idea."

Evan roused from his reverie to chime in.

"Now that we've decided against squatting illegally or ruining our own room," he said. "Let's do something that makes sense and just appeal the decision with the Dean of Student Affairs."

"The Dean Okayed the move herself," said Brad. "The SRC wants us gone, and we can't go over their heads. There aren't any easy solutions."

"This move is happening," said Tarryn. "We'll just have to adjust." This pronouncement was met with silence. After a while, Brad spoke up again.

"Guys, don't let this get you down. We can figure something out further down the line. For now, we have a stall to man. Melvyn, stop digging for your signup sheet, you're not deregistering."

*

That afternoon, the WARP stall was a sorry sight. No-one had bothered to carry all the books, figurines and posters that normally littered the stall. Even Leonard Nimoy looked depressed. Seth was sitting slumped down behind a bare table.

"Any signups?" Brad asked as he approached. Kevin was with him; they were due to take the early afternoon shift together.

"None since I got here," said Seth, shrugging. "There are a few filled in signup sheets lying around though."

"Hopefully the afternoon will go a bit better," said Brad, standing aside to let Seth past before taking his seat. "People have normally given up on the O-Week lectures by then, and their aimlessness makes them vulnerable."

"This is true," said Seth. "And for once it doesn't matter if you tell them where the club-room is." As Seth went on his way, Kevin settled into his chair next to Brad.

"The older guys are taking the news pretty badly," Kevin said once Seth was out of earshot.

"It's understandable," said Brad, shrugging. "WARP is like a second home for a lot of these guys."

"Yeah I know what you mean," said Kevin. "And for Bernard, I'm not sure it's just his second."

Chapter 23

Bernard Kruger: The world has basically ended. When they kick us out of the club-room I'm donating my body to science.
    5 February 2011
    1 Comment: **Nathan Hillary:** Science doesn't have that kind of storage capacity

*

"Do you really think the move will kill the club?" Kevin asked. "Everyone else seems to think so." It was the Wednesday of O-Week, and Brad was walking up to the club-room from the parking lot below the Matrix.

"I'm not sure about killing it," said Brad. "But it will certainly change things."

"It could be a good thing in some ways," said Kevin. "A lot of us would benefit from spending a little less time in WARP. The extra exercise can't hurt either."

"I hope you're right," said Brad as he reached the door to the club-room. "And whatever happens, I won't let WARP die off." He opened the door, and they walked into WARP. Tarryn and Claudia were standing in the middle of the room. Tarryn had her arms crossed and looked annoyed.

"We just want someone to take our shift at the stall so we can take our petition to the Dean of Student Affairs," said Tarryn. "It won't be for very long."

"I'd love to help, but my pants are glued to this chair," said Nathan. He was sitting on an office chair next to the table, while Evan stood next to him, holding a box that was covered with a tablecloth.

"I'm doing data capture," said Seth, who was sitting at the club-room computer.

"This box," said Evan. "I have to uh...hold it." Claudia looked at him in astonishment. He just shrugged. "All the good excuses were taken," he said.

"Everyone relax," said Kevin before the situation could escalate into an argument. "These guys," he continued, gesturing around the room. "Are obviously very busy. I'll take over at the stall until you two get back from the Dean's office."

"Thank you," said Tarryn. "I'm glad someone around here is reasonable." Tarryn and Claudia left together, with Kevin close behind.

"Now that they've left, we can get down to business," Evan said as soon as they were out of the door, putting the box down on the table and whisking off the tablecloth.

"Evan, what's with the cage full of rats?" said Brad, worried.

"Something Bernard said yesterday got me thinking," Evan replied. "It doesn't make sense to make this club-room unfit for habitation, we agree on that. That makes sense. However, if we make the new room uninhabitable, then the SRC can't move us there."

"We made an agreement back in '09," Seth protested. "No more felonies."

"The situation is more serious than you guys realise," said Evan. "That new club-room isn't viable."

"That's a bit of an exaggeration," said Brad. "Sure it's far to walk, but that's not the end of the world."

"It's not just about walking there and back," said Evan. "There's the issue of walking to and from bathrooms."

"Look," said Brad, pulling his bathroom map out of his backpack. "There are bathrooms in the same building. Yes, there are three stories of stairs and a long walk making for a fifteen minute round trip, but it's still pretty bearable." Evan shook his head, pulling out his own bathroom map.

"I have a bit more data than you," he said, pointing to an annotation above the DJ Du Plessis building. Brad leaned over to read the annotation.

'Janitor locks these to take naps inside' it said.

"That IS an issue," said Kevin. "But wrecking the new room is a bit extreme."

"Won't work anyway," added Nathan. "West doesn't shut down buildings just because of rats. If they did, the whole campus would be abandoned."

"But a severe infestation would be a different story," said Evan. "And this is a breed of rats specially bred to reproduce extremely fast for lab-work."

"Still won't work," said Seth. "The Campus Cat Clinic is in the DJ Du Plessis building. Worst building to try start a rat infestation."

"Sorry guys," said Evan, leaning over the cage to address the rats. "It's back to the Med school lab for you."

"How about that petition thing that Tarryn and Claudia are trying?" Brad asked. "Could that work?"

"Not a chance," said Nathan. "West cares even less about petitions than it does about rats."

"Chins up, guys," said Brad. "We'll come up with something. Meanwhile, I'm heading to the stall."

*

"So what's our total for the session?" Kevin asked Brad when Seth arrived at the stall to replace them.

"Got about ten signups," replied Brad. "Not too bad." He grabbed his bag and slung it over his shoulder.

"It really does get tougher as the week goes on," said Kevin, nodding. "You heading back to the clubroom?"

"Afraid not," said Brad. "I have some errands to run." Kevin shrugged.

"I've got some free time," said Kevin. "I'll take a ride with you."

"There's really no need," said Brad. "It's fine."

Kevin raised an eyebrow quizzically.

"You normally hate sitting in traffic by yourself," said Kevin. "What are you up to?"

"It's nothing important," said Brad. "Really."

"In that case, you might as well tell me about it. Come on, I can keep a secret."

"All right," said Brad. "It's pretty embarrassing though, so don't tell anyone in the club." Then he uttered the fateful words: "So there's this girl, right..."

*

"We've all done some dumb stuff over girls," said Kevin. "But I have to commend your commitment." Brad shrugged. They were outside a bulk liquor store, loading crates of beer into Brad's car.

"No-one wants to be the guy correcting people over small details," said Brad. "That's why I didn't say anything at first. It didn't seem like it mattered at the time, so I just went with it."

"You really think you can run a bar by yourself, and still find time to go talk to this girl?" Kevin asked.

"It'll be pretty tough, but I think I can pull it off," said Brad. "If she doesn't stop by the War-Games room I'll close up early and go find her."

"Tell you what," said Kevin. "Cut me in for half the take from the bar and I'll help you out."

"You'd do that for me?" said Brad. Kevin shrugged.

"Sure thing," he said. "I could use the money. Not to mention, those fridges you mentioned could be handy with all the blackouts in my neighbourhood lately."

*

It was around 6PM that Brad and Kevin crossed the Amic deck onto West Campus. They found the area around Science Stadium transformed in preparation for the Sports Council Street Party. Temporary metal barriers had been erected to restrict access except at one entry gate. At the North end of the road, a stage had been set up on the road outside the row of club-rooms and the clubs were all setting up makeshift bars outside their rooms.

"You ever been to one of these parties before?" Kevin asked as they made their way down towards the War-Games room.

"Nope," said Brad. "You?"

"Once," said Kevin, grimacing. "I met Tara at an O-Week Vodka party. Then I got lost trying to find a bathroom while blind drunk. By the time I found my way back, she was making out with Bernard."

"It's like you dodged a bullet," Brad commented. "But then spent the next six months tracking down that bullet and fighting off another guy just for the opportunity to jump back in front of it."

"That girl over there, waving," said Kevin, quickly changing the subject. "Is that Karen?" Brad turned and looked where Kevin was pointing. Karen was making her way over from the Rowing Club bar, smiling broadly.

"Totally worth it," Kevin said under his breath.

"Hi Karen," Brad said nervously as she enfolded him in a familiar hug.

"Jamie!'" she said. "I'm glad you made it."

"So am I," said Brad. "I left home at 6am but you never know with traffic these days. This is Kevin, by the way. He's helping me out with the bar tonight."

"I'm Vice-President of War-Games," Kevin added. "I actually won the election but I let Brad here take the reins," he continued. Brad shot him a loaded glance.

"That's very generous of you," said Karen, reaching out to shake his hand. "Nice to meet you, by the way."

"It's lovely to meet you too," said Kevin. "But forget this 'Jamie' thing. In these parts, we call him Brad. It's short for Bradford."

"Oh, I see," said Karen. "That makes tons of sense. Well, don't let me keep you. This zoo is opening in half an hour and you guys have a bar to set up!"

"I'll go take care of that," said Kevin. "Karen, you keep Brad busy; I don't want him getting in my way," he continued, grinning.

"So, Bradford, huh?" said Karen. "How did they come up with that one?"

"I wish I knew," said Brad. "I'm pretty sure that James just got my name wrong and didn't want to admit it."

*

Chapter 24

Aristos Hadjigeorgio: 'Try everything you can think of. Take credit for whatever works' – Buddha
6 February 2012

*

"Brad, you have to check this out," said Kevin. Brad kicked his legs to free himself from his sleeping bag. They were in the War-Games room. Brad hadn't been expecting to sleep in the room, but he had prepared for the possibility.

"What's up?" Brad asked, his voice hoarse and sleepy.

"Did you take a break from getting cosy with Karen to stop and count the money at any point last night?" Kevin asked. Brad shook his head.

"Should I have?" he asked. "Look, don't worry too much about it. I honestly expected to make a bit of a loss on this."

"That's not the problem," said Kevin. "I'm just trying to figure out if we have to pay tax on this." Brad sat up and stared at him.

"What?" Brad asked. "We can't have made that much."

"We sold out of beer, Brad," said Kevin. "Then I went and bought some bottles of liqueur from Fencing club. I sold it along with that ice-cream I was storing in the freezer here while my power's out at home. With how hot it was yesterday, the stuff sold like crazy."

"Nice work," said Brad appreciatively. "We pulled this off and even managed to turn a profit," he said.

"Must be karma compensating for losing the clubroom," said Kevin. "And by that logic, nothing can go wrong for a while."

"So much for that logic then," said Brad. "I just got this message from Karen."

"She's not interested?" asked Kevin. "Or are you condemned to the friendzone?"

"Worse," said Brad. "She says she's really looking forward to working with me at Sports Council meetings. Apparently all the sports club executives meet every second week."

"That's pretty bad," said Kevin. "You have a plan?"

"I dunno," said Brad. "Just showing up at the meetings probably won't work. I assume that the Sports Council will have a list of everyone who should be there."

"Problem for later," said Kevin. "For now, I really need to get to the Sports Hall and take a shower." After Kevin left, Brad sat with his head in his hands for a while, trying to figure out how to explain things to Karen.

"When in doubt, escalate," he said to himself, picking up his phone as he finally decided on a course of action.

"Hey, it's Brad. We need to talk," he said.

"Sure thing," said Evan. "But I must warn you I'm as hung over as you sound. Some guy who looks like Kevin sold me a shit-ton of liqueur and ice-cream last night."

"Happens to the best of us," said Brad. "Now, the favour I'm asking is going to sound really strange, but just hear me out."

"Go ahead," said Evan.

"I need to rope in a bunch of WARP guys to join the War-Games club and call for a new election to vote me in as president," said Brad, feeling a bit breathless and nervous as he waited for Evan's reply. The other side of the line was silent, and Brad began to pace the room as his tension built. "Evan, you still there?" Brad asked.

"Yeah, I'm here," said Evan. "You say you want us to get War-Games reinstated as a club?" Evan asked, sounding thoughtful.

"That's what I'm asking," said Brad. Brad tapped his foot impatiently as Evan lapsed back into thought.

"Brad," he said. "That's absolutely brilliant."

"Look, I know it's a lot to ask but," Brad started before fully processing what Evan had said. "I mean, yeah. Brilliant."

"Of course we're on board," Evan continued, excitement rising in his voice. "I'm gonna call everyone and we can get on this." Brad sat back down on an office chair, utterly confused. Still, it seemed to have worked, so he settled in to type a message to Karen.

'I couldn't be more excited about it!' he typed. 'I had an amazing time hanging out with you last night.' As he waited for a reply, Kevin walked into the room wearing a bathrobe and flip-flops. He had a puzzled look on his face and his hair was still wet from the shower.

"I just got a text from Evan," he said. "He says that you saved WARP."

*

Hand-drawn on the whiteboard in WARP was a scale map of the campus, highlighting the walking routes to WARP and to the new room. Brad guessed it was Seth who had drawn it at some point. The club-room was packed with regulars who had come in for Evan's emergency meeting, but the noises of the crowd mostly washed over Brad. He was leaning back in a chair behind the table, trying to focus on what Evan was saying. Brad had woken up still flush with giddy thoughts of Karen, but as the morning wore on the effects of the previous night had begun to make themselves felt. He had managed only three hours of fitful sleep on the War-Games couch and Nino's wasn't open yet, so his mind was blanketed in a thick pre-coffee fog.

"Listen up everybody," Evan was saying. He was standing in front of the map on the whiteboard, with a marker in his hand. "You can see we've been brainstorming solutions to the clubroom issue," he continued, waving at a collection of scrawled notes in a variety of handwriting. 'Webcam lectures' said one of them. 'Zip-line?' said another. "These ideas are all bad," Evan continued. "So it's fortunate that Brad has stepped up as president and come up with a workable solution. If enough of us join the War-Games club, we can elect ourselves as their Executive Committee," Evan paused to mark a large X on the map. "As you can see, War-Games

"I just got a text from Evan," he said. "He says that you saved WARP."

*

Hand-drawn on the whiteboard in WARP was a scale map of the campus, highlighting the walking routes to WARP and to the new room. Brad guessed it was Seth who had drawn it at some point. The club-room was packed with regulars who had come in for Evan's emergency meeting, but the noises of the crowd mostly washed over Brad. He was leaning back in a chair behind the table, trying to focus on what Evan was saying. Brad had woken up still flush with giddy thoughts of Karen, but as the morning wore on the effects of the previous night had begun to make themselves felt. He had managed only three hours of fitful sleep on the War-Games couch and Nino's wasn't open yet, so his mind was blanketed in a thick pre-coffee fog.

"Listen up everybody," Evan was saying. He was standing in front of the map on the whiteboard, with a marker in his hand. "You can see we've been brainstorming solutions to the clubroom issue," he continued, waving at a collection of scrawled notes in a variety of handwriting. 'Webcam lectures' said one of them. 'Zip-line?' said another. "These ideas are all bad," Evan continued. "So it's fortunate that Brad has stepped up as president and come up with a workable solution. If enough of us join the War-Games club, we can elect ourselves as their Executive Committee," Evan paused to mark a large X on the map. "As you can see, War-Games

"Happens to the best of us," said Brad. "Now, the favour I'm asking is going to sound really strange, but just hear me out."

"Go ahead," said Evan.

"I need to rope in a bunch of WARP guys to join the War-Games club and call for a new election to vote me in as president," said Brad, feeling a bit breathless and nervous as he waited for Evan's reply. The other side of the line was silent, and Brad began to pace the room as his tension built. "Evan, you still there?" Brad asked.

"Yeah, I'm here," said Evan. "You say you want us to get War-Games reinstated as a club?" Evan asked, sounding thoughtful.

"That's what I'm asking," said Brad. Brad tapped his foot impatiently as Evan lapsed back into thought.

"Brad," he said. "That's absolutely brilliant."

"Look, I know it's a lot to ask but," Brad started before fully processing what Evan had said. "I mean, yeah. Brilliant."

"Of course we're on board," Evan continued, excitement rising in his voice. "I'm gonna call everyone and we can get on this." Brad sat back down on an office chair, utterly confused. Still, it seemed to have worked, so he settled in to type a message to Karen.

'I couldn't be more excited about it!' he typed. 'I had an amazing time hanging out with you last night.' As he waited for a reply, Kevin walked into the room wearing a bathrobe and flip-flops. He had a puzzled look on his face and his hair was still wet from the shower.

is in a decent location. For Engineering and Law students, it's actually closer than WARP. Once we've taken over, we can just move WARP into that club-room."

Applause rippled through the club-room, and Brad inclined his head in acknowledgment. He stood there dazed as Ari shook him vigorously by the hand and Bernard slapped him on the back in congratulations. Looking around the room, he saw Tarryn smiling at him from where she was standing near the door. Claudia flashed him a thumbs up and a warm smile. Seth, sitting to Brad's left, was entering the new location on Google Maps to calculate walking distances from important locations on campus. Liking what he saw, he nodded in Brad's direction.

"I'm actually impressed," James said from the other side of the table. "I have taught you well."

Kevin leaned in close from where he was sitting to Brad's right.

"Remember to make me Vice-President," Kevin whispered, grinning. "And no-one else needs to know this was just an accident."

"Fair enough," said Brad. "Now let's go see if Nino's is open." As Brad was walking through the door he heard Melvyn's voice, sounding puzzled.

"Why is there a pair of pants glued to this chair?"

Chapter 25

Nathan Hillary: I know that I won't achieve my goals in life because there aren't any time travellers trying to stop me.
     13 February 2012

*

"It's amazing what they'll let you get away with," James was saying as he typed at the WARP PC. "You're sure that name changes take twenty four hours to take effect?"

Brad wasn't paying much attention. He was sitting on a couch, intent on his phone. It was Valentine's day and that night would mark his third date with Karen. It seemed a perfect opportunity to ask her to make their relationship official, and he had a feeling the answer would be yes.

"Seth?" James asked. "I need to be sure, the timing here has to be precise."

"I was just checking it," Seth replied. "And yeah, it's twenty four hours."

"Good thing I put it through early," said James. "There's a bit of leeway, since people will still be asleep when it goes through." Brad tuned out their conversation and went back to thinking about how to answer Karen's text. 'Can't wait to see you tonight! I have a surprise in store ;)'

Brad had never really gotten to grips with emoticons.

Do I send back a smiley face? Brad thought to himself. *Or do I stick to my usual style? Do I try to be witty, or do I say something nice?* The text he'd typed out read 'If the surprise is a younger brother coming with on our date, then some 90s sitcoms will be calling about getting their premise back.'

"Don't send that," said Kevin, looking over Brad's shoulder from a chair behind the couch.

"Why not?" Brad asked. "It's clever."

"Before you say anything, ask yourself 'Would Nathan say this?' If the answer is yes, then don't say it," said Kevin. Brad nodded slowly, seeing the wisdom in this advice.

"You're probably right," said Brad, backspacing rapidly. "I'll just tell her I'm excited to see what it is, and throw on a smiley face."

"Perfect," said Kevin. "Don't over-think these things. Keep it casual."

"Thanks for the help," said Brad. "Now wish me luck. I'm stopping off at home to shower and get fancy, then I'm heading off."

*

"Surprise!" said Karen. "This is my little brother, Dennis." Brad managed a crooked smile and extended a hand in greeting.

"Hi," said Brad. "Nice to meet you, I'm Brad." He then turned to Karen and said "I thought it was just going to be me and you. Not that it's a problem of course," he added hastily, not wanting to offend. "It's great that your brother is here."

"Well at least I know you're a bad liar," Karen said, laughing. "Relax, this isn't my brother. He's one of the waiters. I was just messing with you." Brad sighed, feeling relieved as Dennis walked off.

"I should have noticed the uniform," said Brad, pulling out a chair. They were at Gino's, the pizzeria where they had first met. "You know," he added, grinning ruefully. "You're going to fit right in with the WARP group."

"I guess I'll take that as a compliment," Karen said. "I take it they're big on pranks there?"

"Oh yes," said Brad. "Just today James was changing someone's name on their Facebook account. There will be quite a surprise waiting for them when they log on tomorrow morning."

"You never did tell me how you ended up president of two different clubs," Karen asked, looking across the table at Brad.

"That's a story for another time," said Brad. "Speaking of Faceboook, though," he continued nervously. "I was thinking of changing my relationship status." Karen sat up a bit straighter before she responded.

"Changing it to what?" she asked. Brad's confidence grew as he began to realise that she looked excited and a little nervous.

"In a relationship," he said. "With you," he added. Karen took a deep breath and looked Brad right in the eyes.

"I would like that a lot," she said with a broad smile. "And I think I'll do the same." Brad smiled back at her.

"I think that's news worthy of some champagne," he said. "Let me see if I can get us a waiter," he continued, raising his hand for attention.

"Hi," a waiter said, walking up to their table. "My name is Dennis and I'll be your waiter tonight."

*

Jamie 'Bradford' Rogers is now in a relationship with **No-one because he's a loser**

15 February 2012

3 comments: **James Green**: I hope you're very happy together.
No-one because he's a loser: Looks like my account has been hacked, and it's taking a while to change my name back. I can vouch that Brad is in a relationship with a real girl and he's not a loser. His friends are.
James Green: Shame on you Brad, letting your imaginary girlfriend fight your battles for you.

www.ingramcontent.com/pod-product-compliance
Lightning Source LLC
Chambersburg PA
CBHW061323040426
42444CB00011B/2756